T0156899

The Flight Connection

MARY R. RODGERS

WESTBOW°
PRESS
A DIVISION OF THOMAS NELSON
& ZONDERVAN

This is a work of fiction. Names, characters, places, and incidents are either the product of the author's imagination or are used fictitiously, and any resemblance to any actual persons, living or dead, events, or locales is entirely coincidental.

WestBow Press books may be ordered through booksellers or by contacting:

WestBow Press
A Division of Thomas Nelson & Zondervan
1663 Liberty Drive
Bloomington, IN 47403
www.westbowpress.com
1 (866) 928-1240

Because of the dynamic nature of the Internet, any web addresses or links contained in this book may have changed since publication and may no longer be valid. The views expressed in this work are solely those of the author and do not necessarily reflect the views of the publisher, and the publisher hereby disclaims any responsibility for them.

Any people depicted in stock imagery provided by Thinkstock are models, and such images are being used for illustrative purposes only. Certain stock imagery © Thinkstock.

ISBN: 978-1-4908-8206-2 (sc)
ISBN: 978-1-4908-8207-9 (hc)
ISBN: 978-1-4908-8205-5 (e)

Print information available on the last page.

Library of Congress Control Number: 2015908639

WestBow Press rev. date: 06/18/2015

Contents

To God for touching my heart and allowing me to receive the passion to write. To my precious family for supporting me and allowing me the time necessary to fulfill this passion and dream.

And last but not least, to all those who are lost or going through circumstances they do not understand. Sometimes it takes a lifetime to fully comprehend the reason for our challenges—if in fact we ever do understand.

We all have a story. Remember you are never alone.

Prologue

Sometimes the most wonderful and unbelievable things happen when we least expect them. You just can't help but believe that with God all things are possible.

It was just another day for both Cynthia and Mason. They were both preparing to embark on yet another lonely business trip.

Little did either of them know just how much their lives were about to change by the time they reached their respective destinations.

How was it that two absolute strangers could have drawn so close to each other in just a matter of hours?

How could they both feel that quite possibly they had fallen in love?

Was it even possible?

Chapter 1

Prepare for Takeoff

*A*t *least it's a beautiful, clear, warm, California day*, Cynthia thought.

Who could complain about eighty-two-degree weather? May weather in California was almost always nice weather, but today was exceptionally nice. *A great day to fly halfway around the world*, she concluded.

Cynthia usually made it a point to leave for her business trips on Sunday afternoon in order to arrive at the office in Milan on Tuesday morning. However, on this trip she decided to leave on Saturday so she could arrive in Milan on Sunday afternoon, get a good night's rest, and show up in the office on Monday morning instead.

She wanted to be back home by Thursday so she could get some rest before helping out with her church's Memorial Day outreach and family picnic that was scheduled to take place on the Saturday after she arrived back home.

The annual outreach was a huge community event that Cynthia had volunteered to manage for the past three years.

Today, she would have been more than happy to drive herself to the airport and pay for the daily parking. Her company would have gladly covered the expense. It was much less expensive than taking a taxi.

Driving herself to the airport would have given her the luxury of taking her time when she returned from the trip to claim her bags and get to her car instead of having to rush, knowing that someone was waiting on her.

However, as usual, it turned out that Dan Reed, an old friend of her husband, Jack, wouldn't have it any other way when he offered to take her to the airport and pick her up on Thursday as well.

Since Jack had passed away more than four years ago, Dan had taken it upon himself to take care of her and her son, Bryce, whether they needed it or not.

Dan never took "No, thank you" or even just a flat-out *no* for an answer.

That trait had definitely driven Cynthia and sometimes even Bryce to the point of extreme frustration and annoyance, but they both knew Dan always meant well.

He had been so sweet and thoughtful since Jack's accident. But he seemed almost obsessed with it, and she wished that he would allow her and Bryce some space and that he would get a life of his own.

She had spent the past few years trying to find a way to ask him to back off without hurting his feelings.

Dan pulled up to the curb at Terminal 4 at LAX for departures, and as he opened his door to get out, he said, "Okay, now I will pick you up on Thursday at curbside. Be careful. Don't be too trusting, and if you need me for anything, give me a call."

"I'll be fine Dan. Thank you for the ride," Cynthia replied.

"Now give me a hug." Cynthia obediently returned his hug.

"Bye. See you Thursday," she said as she grabbed her bags and walked into the terminal.

She always felt so smothered when Dan treated her like she was helpless. She almost instantly felt better as she walked away.

Cynthia walked up to the check-in desk and gave the attendant her ticket information.

She put her suitcase on the scale and was glad that she did not exceed the fifty-pound limit. She almost always packs more than she needs, but the fear of leaving something behind that she might need overwhelms her.

The attendant handed Cynthia her boarding pass.

"Thank you," Cynthia said.

"You're welcome. Your gate is to your left and just around the corner. Enjoy your flight," the attendant replied.

Cynthia proceeded toward the security checkpoint and gate as directed.

She went through security without having to be searched. *What a relief,* she thought. For some reason she was always selected to be searched and patted down. Maybe she was just being a little sensitive, but she was sure it happened more often than not.

Aside from the empty, lonely feeling she always felt when she was traveling so far away for business, everything was great. *How many people get to fly to Italy in May on the company's dime?* she would think to herself in order to get some form of comfort, however little comfort it might be.

Although her eighteen-year-old son was enjoying his freedom at college away from home and would not even notice her gone, she still felt like she was leaving her baby behind.

No matter what she did or told herself to bring comfort, she would always tear up. It was a little embarrassing, she knew.

Ten and a half hours on an airplane, sitting so close to someone you've never met and would never see again, what fun! she thought sarcastically.

Cynthia was sure she had already seen all the movies that they would offer on the flight or that she would actually want to take the time to watch. Many of them were just not the old corny, wholesome, unbelievable romances she loved to watch. Puzzles, books, and magazines were her only hope to get through this trip.

Alone again— So what's new?

On the positive side she could spend time reading her Bible and meditating on verses that gave her so much comfort and strength. She could pray silently to her best friend, her precious Savior, whom she had grown so close to throughout her life.

She had always had so much to pray for, and she was oh-so-grateful for having the privilege to do so.

Cynthia looked at her boarding pass.

"Cynthia Ann Stewart. Row 20A," she read. It was a window seat. She always did her best to make sure she booked a window seat so that she could try to sleep as comfortably as possible.

Boarding time is at 3:20 p.m. Cynthia was always good about getting to the airport in plenty of time. She always tried to arrive at the airport at least two and a half hours before her departure time, which today is at 3:50 p.m. She still had another hour to go before boarding time.

While Cynthia sat waiting at her gate, she thought she would try to sleep as much as she could from the moment the flight took off until around four hours or so into the flight.

She stayed up packing almost all night and was starting to feel tired.

It would be about 2:00 a.m. in Milan when the airplane finally took off. She wanted to try to adjust to the time difference as much as possible before landing in Milan.

"Mason Thomas Scott. Row 20C," he read as he glanced at his boarding pass. *Not too bad, an aisle seat*, he thought. He could get up and stretch anytime he wanted to without disturbing anybody.

Here I go again, another trip, he thought. *How can I be getting ready to take off again?* He had just gotten back from New York only two weeks ago! *Bills have to get paid and things have to get done somehow, I guess.*

Mason always felt so alone on these trips. *Italy*, he thought sadly.

His wife, Lilly, would have loved to see Italy, especially Rome, perhaps even Venice and Milan. He would have taken her anywhere she wanted to go.

He missed her so much. *How could it be eighteen months since she was taken from me?* It had been so long.

He had been so busy getting his son, Thomas, through the loss of his mother. The time just flew by.

The terminal was quite crowded. *Where do these families get the money to travel to and from Europe or anywhere else for that matter? Some of these families have two or three children and don't look or act like it's their first time traveling.*

This made Mason think how much he would love to bring his son Tommy on a trip like this. He would definitely suggest it to Tom for next year before he finds someone and gets married. *Just us guys*, Mason thought.

Oh, no! Mason noticed a couple of babies. Both looked just under a year old. *I don't have anything against babies,* he thought, *but being seated just inches from a tired, cranky baby or toddler on an eleven-hour flight will not be fun at all.* He knew from experience.

"Please, Lord, help me out here," he whispered softly.

"Now boarding rows six through ten," the flight attendant announced.

"Well, here I go," Cynthia said softly to herself.

Earlier Cynthia called Bryce to let him know she was boarding and that he should call his Aunt Sara if anything urgent came up.

She had already let her sister know she would be traveling to Europe and that Bryce would call her if she could not be reached and something urgent came up.

Sara was always so sweet with stepping in to help out. She was the perfect big sister. Cynthia loved her so much.

"Okay, sweetie, I love you too. I miss you already. Bye, bye, sweetie." Cynthia ended the call and put her cell phone in her purse.

She felt a burning sensation in her nostrils as she once again began to tear up. "Oh, come on, Cynthia! Get a grip," she told herself as she dried her tears.

She grabbed her things and headed for the gate attendant.

She politely greeted the flight attendant at the entrance of the plane. She always hated the walk down the aisle to her seat. It never seemed wide enough. She carefully carried her carry-on close to her so she didn't bump it against anyone. She hoped she would make it all the way to row twenty without causing injury to anyone.

"Great! Here we are—row twenty."

No one was seated in her row yet. She was the first one. Hopefully she would have enough time to throw her carry-on in the overhead compartment and get settled in and as comfortable as possible in her seat before the other two passengers arrived.

Cynthia quickly threw her small briefcase on her seat. This was her most important case, her survival kit. She had a laptop inside, a few magazines, a writing pad, her Bible, and a very nice variety of snacks that included the cannot-live-without box of circus animal cookies. She made sure to place an extra box of these never-do-without cookies in her check-in bag for the flight home.

Next she went to lift up her carry-on. This was always a bit of a challenge, as it was packed to its maximum capacity with things she knew she must have in order to survive a weeklong trip. And of course, it also contained some of the materials she needed to review for her meetings. As usual she was struggling to get it in the overhead.

"Can I help you with that?" she heard a voice just behind her.

"Oh, sure, thank you. Thank you so much", she replied.

A very nice gentleman took her bag and very quickly and easily placed it nicely in the overhead compartment right over her row.

"There you go," he said with a smile.

"Thanks again," Cynthia said with sincere appreciation and a big smile.

She had always been blessed with angels helping her out from time to time. That was what she called the many kind people that helped her throughout her life—*angels*. They just showed up out of nowhere at just the right time. She was sure God sent them just for her. This always made her smile.

Cynthia settled in to her seat and waited to see who she would be sharing row twenty with for the next ten hours or so.

It looked like the two infants she had seen earlier were behind her several rows back. She was always amazed at how well most infants and toddlers traveled. Some parents did exceptionally well with their little ones. They are so adorable, innocent, and sweet. She loved babies. Cynthia would volunteer to work in the nursery at her church from time to time. She really enjoyed being around children.

Well, she thought happily, *still no one in 20B or 20C, and the flight leaves in ten minutes. I just might have row twenty all to myself.*

I could stretch out, jump from window to aisle seat. Wouldn't that be great! That would surely make it a first-class trip—that is, if another passenger didn't notice the empty seat and snag it for themselves.

Thomas was a very independent young man of twenty. He loved college life. But even so, he and his dad grew much closer this past year and a half since his mom had passed. They were bound and determined to take care of each other.

Mason loved every opportunity to talk with his precious son. He was talking to Tom when he heard the final boarding call.

"Oh, man, Tommy, I have to go! I love you too, son. Take care and see you soon. Bye." Mason walked quickly to the gate entrance and handed the attendant his ticket.

As he stepped into the airplane, he noticed that he wasn't the last person to board, although the plane was almost all boarded and filled to capacity.

He looked toward the direction of where row twenty would be and thought, *Wow, just one person in the window seat. No one in the middle seat yet. I guess I'm not that late.*

When Mason arrived at row twenty, Cynthia turned toward him. "Hi," he said.

"Hi," she replied.

Good. She doesn't seem like much of a talker, Mason thought to himself.

He liked sitting by polite, quiet people who would rather keep to themselves without feeling the need to chat. She looked just like one of those quiet types.

Now let's see who we get in seat 20B. That is the determining factor of how this trip will play out, he thought. *Poor lady was probably hoping for the entire row. I know I would have been hoping.*

He made sure he had all his reading materials and laptop with him. Unfortunately he could not find space for his carry-on near his row. He had to place his bag in an overhead compartment a few rows back.

I guess that's the price of waiting until the last minute to board, he thought. *Oh, well.* He would have plenty of time between his connections in London to grab his bag. No worries.

The gentleman seated in the seat behind him looked up at him. He had an angry look on his face. His eyes locked onto Mason's, and he just stared.

"Hi," Mason said with a smile.

The man just shook his head and turned away.

Mason just shook it off as just someone having a bad day.

"God, please send your love and peace to this dear gentleman. In Jesus' name, amen," Mason prayed silently.

Mason then settled into his seat, put his seat belt on, and prepared for takeoff. This was going to be the farthest and longest he had been away from Tommy since his mother had passed.

The flight attendant announced that they were closing the doors and preparing for takeoff. *What a break. No one in 20B. Thank you, Lord!*

Mason made sure he packed his study Bible. That was the best thing about these long flights. It gave him time to catch up with his Bible reading. He also had to prepare for his meeting on Monday morning, and he would have plenty of time to do that as well. It should be a pretty busy flight. He hoped time would just fly by.

The flight attendant closed the door and announced for all passengers to please buckle their seat belts and to turn off all electronic devices. She did their usual live demonstration of what to do in case of an emergency. The airplane began to taxi to its position in line for takeoff.

After about ten minutes the airplane began to accelerate. The plane shook as the speed increased. Then came the pull on liftoff.

Well, we are on our way. Cynthia figured that she would read a little until the first beverage service. The pillow and blanket were neatly stacked on her briefcase underneath her seat. She thought she would read a few magazines and maybe watch a movie afterward.

The gentlemen sitting next to her seemed very nice. He was probably on a business trip as well. She was so glad the middle seat was not filled. *I hope he is willing to share it.*

Mason looked at her and smiled. As if reading her mind, he said, "It's all yours if you'd like."

Oh, my goodness, how sweet, she thought.

She smiled shyly back at Mason and said, "Well, thank you. That's very nice of you, but we can share it. It's going to be a very long flight, you know."

"It's a deal," he said with a smile and turned away respectfully.

Great! Mason thought. *A very thoughtful row mate.* He couldn't ask for more. She seemed very nice. *I wonder what her story is*, Mason thought.

He was always curious about people he found interesting, kind or rude. Just like the gentleman sitting behind him. He wondered why he seemed so angry.

Mason considered himself a bit of a private person, so he would never inquire or probe into other people's lives. He was, however, a great listener if people needed or wanted to talk, vent, or share. He considered himself a great confidant.

He pulled out his Kindle and searched for a book to read. He figured he would start it and see where it went. He really wasn't much of a reader of fiction. He enjoyed books on history and religion the best. He read for a while.

The woman next to him sat quietly in her seat, browsing through the airline magazines. He noticed most of the passengers were also settling themselves down for the long flight.

About thirty minutes into their flight a flight attendant announced that they were preparing for the first beverage service.

Finally, Mason thought. He would order a ginger ale, take a couple of aspirins, read a bit more, and try to sleep some. He had endured a nagging headache all morning, and it was still lingering.

He didn't sleep well last night, and he had been running around all day, taking care of last-minute errands. All he wanted to do now was relax and close his eyes for a while.

Mason took out his Bible to read over a few chapters that brought him the most comfort. He had to admit he really felt lonely for Tommy. He had made him his whole world in the last year and a half. He glanced over and noticed the woman next to him took out a devotional. She glanced up and saw him glancing at it.

When their eyes met, he smiled and asked, "Are you a believer?"

"Yes," she answered with a smile. "Are you?"

"You bet," he said.

"I have always believed that there was a God, but only have come to really know him in the last eight years," Cynthia shared.

"My mother was a Christian as long as I could remember and I have considered myself one all my life. But like you, I have grown to know him much more as time passes," Mason replied. "So where do you go to church?"

"I go to Crossroads Church located about thirty minutes from Los Angeles and about ten minutes from my house. We have about two thousand members. It's been my home church for the past six years. I absolutely love it. And where do you go to church?"

"I attend Living Water Church about an hour east of Los Angeles, not too far from where I live. We have about twelve thousand members. It is what is known as a mega church. We have so many activities and interest groups that make it seem very cozy. There are a lot of opportunities to get to know a lot of fellow believers. It's a very fun and exciting place."

"Knowing the Lord has definitely been the best thing in my life. He has brought me through things that I know I could not have made it through on my own."

"Same here, most definitely. I will have to give you an Amen to that for sure"

"Well let me let you get back to your book." Cynthia said with a smile.

"No problem, it was nice chatting with you." Mason felt so comfortable, sitting next to a fellow believer. He loved to talk about the Lord.

The flight attendants were quickly approaching with the beverages. Cynthia wasn't quite sure whether she should have coffee to help keep her up or juice.

"Would you like something to drink?" the attendant asked Cynthia first.

"Yes, apple juice please," she decided. The attendant handed the drink and a small package of pretzels to her.

"Thank you," said Cynthia.

"You're welcome," the attendant replied.

"And for you, sir?" the attendant asked Mason.

"Ginger ale please," Mason replied. After the attendant handed him his drink, he reached into his jacket pocket and took out a couple of aspirins he had put there earlier.

Cynthia stayed awake as long as she could. The man beside her was out cold. His soft, peaceful snoring began to make her very sleepy. She pulled out her pillow from underneath her seat and pulled the blanket over her shoulders. About two hours into the flight she finally dosed off.

Chapter 2

The Flight Plan

Mason and Cynthia were awakened by the sound of clanging dishes and the smell of freshly brewed coffee. The flight attendants were beginning to serve dinner.

"Good evening," Mason said to Cynthia with a tired smile as he unbuckled his seat belt and stood to head to the restroom.

"Good evening," Cynthia replied shyly.

She felt a little self-conscience, as she wondered what she must look like. She immediately grabbed her cosmetic bag and headed for the restroom as well.

She never liked to bother the other passengers with having to get up and use the restroom, so she always made it a point to go when they did if she could. She wanted to hurry up and make it back before the flight attendants made it to her row to serve their meals.

When she got back to her seat, Mason had already returned. He immediately got up when he saw her and allowed her to take her seat.

"Thank you," Cynthia said.

"No problem," replied Mason.

Just in time. Dinner was just two rows ahead.

The flight attendant first handed Cynthia her plate and asked if she would like some coffee.

"Oh, yes, please," she replied.

Cynthia was an avid coffee drinker. She called it her life's blood, especially first thing in the morning, but for now she would use it to stay awake as much as possible. She was glad the dinner tray included a small bottle of water as well because flying made her very thirsty.

The flight attendant then handed Mason his meal and asked, "And you, sir? Would you like some coffee?"

"Yes, thank you," Mason replied.

They both prayed softly to themselves before they started eating.

"Not bad … for airplane food," Mason started. Cynthia smiled and agreed.

"Better than going hungry—that's for sure," Cynthia replied.

"So do you have a testimony?" Mason asked with a smile.

"My life is a testimony," Cynthia replied. "And how about you?"

"Same here," Mason replied with an even bigger smile.

He could not believe how intrusive he was or how comfortable he felt talking to her. It must have been the connection they have with their faith. That always made him feel comfortable with people he just met, knowing they had something in common. And she was definitely very easy to talk to.

They both continued with their meals.

The flight attendants began making their rounds to pick up plates and trash. After their plates were picked up, both Cynthia and Mason thought about what to do next. Read, work on their laptops, perhaps watch a movie—all seemed mundane to both of them.

They both wanted to stay awake as long as possible to try to adjust to the time zone at their respective destinations. It was currently around 8:00 a.m. in Italy.

"So going back to our testimonies, would you like to share yours?" Mason asked daringly with a smile. He himself didn't know where that question came from.

His daring smile was quickly replaced by a wide-eyed, surprised, almost sorry look. What was he thinking? He only met this woman about six hours ago. He didn't even know her name.

As expected, Cynthia looked a little surprised. But she sensed his discomfort after he asked the question. She found it a little cute and funny. The expression on his face was hilarious. She had to laugh.

"Well, if you are up to it, I would like to make an even better suggestion that will make this flight just fly by," Cynthia replied playfully.

So glad she wasn't completely offended or uncomfortable with his very inconsiderate, bold question, which she very much looked surprised by, he replied curiously, "What would that be?"

"Why don't we share our whole lives from our first memory until this minute? Well, maybe not every detail of our lives since we only have around four or five hours left, but the big parts. The parts that make us who we are today or what we remember the most that we can attribute to what made us into the people we are," she continued. "Basically, our lives in a nutshell."

"Sounds interesting," he said.

"I mean, we are never going to see each other again, so we can be very open. It can be like therapy."

Both chuckled mischievously as Mason took over a bit.

"Okay, rules of the game are no questions, no interruptions, and we break it down like so: first memory to junior high school, high school to college, and after college to the present day," Mason started.

"We each get about thirty to forty-five minutes for each subject. That's about four or five hour's total. About two and a half hours each," Mason continued. "What do you think?"

"Sounds like a plan," Cynthia replied in agreement. *What did I just get mself into?* she thought. *Oh well, it will surely pass the time away.* They would be in London before they knew it—that was for sure.

Mason asked suggestively, "Lady's first?"

"Sure," replied Cynthia.

Chapter 3

First Memory to Junior High School—Cynthia

Okay, let's see. I was born Cynthia Ann Langston. I grew up in a small urban city about twenty minutes outside of Los Angeles. My first memory is riding in my father's huge truck up a dirt road that led up to our house. I was the apple of his eye. I would follow him everywhere. There was nothing I could do wrong in his eyes to my mother's dismay.

"Cynthia! Sit still!" my mother yelled as she tugged on my hair.

I remember my mom pulling my hair so hard and fastening a rubber band around it so tight my eyes would almost close. She brushed it so hard. I dreaded the daily ritual. I was around four and a half. This is my strongest first memory. This lasted until I was able to satisfy her with my ability to do my own hair, which I worked very hard to do.

I had a brother and a sister. Both were from a different father, my mother's first husband. It turns out my mother divorced her first husband while she was pregnant with me.

My dad also divorced his wife during that same period. My dad did not have any other children. I was his first and only child. Hence, the apple of his eye. Pretty controversial stuff for that day and age.

My parents argued a lot, and we kids were always terrified and scared. Sometimes it would get physical … between them and with us. Actually it was our mother who was physically abusive, my father just verbally. It was usually due to excessive alcohol consumption or the aftereffects.

Jared was the oldest of the three of us. He was eight, a little more than four years older than me. Sara was six. They were both lonely for their dad.

My dad didn't really treat them well. The typical stepfather, he barely put up with them.

Their dad was nice but preoccupied with his new life. He had a new home, a new wife, and a new baby girl.

My parents both went to church from time to time. Their church attendance was more of a ritual than spiritual. It seemed to me at the time that church was just a thing you had to do. I really didn't know why we went. They observed some of the rituals, but truly I didn't know exactly what was going on.

It didn't seem to help with the things that were going on in our home. But somehow looking back, I always felt I was being watched over. God was truly with me, with us all really.

My mother would create scriptures of her own sometimes, some that sounded pretty convincing. She usually used them to cut down, condemn, and rebuke people. She was very self-righteous.

Believing in God didn't seem like it was very loving or a kind thing to me. It seemed like more of a weapon. The only thing my mother clearly communicated was that if you weren't good, God would punish you.

Oh yes, she also said that the Devil would scratch our feet at night if we weren't good. To this day, I will not let my feet stray out of the covers while I am sleeping—unless I'm wearing a thick pair of socks. I never really know exactly whether I meet up with God's standards for being good for the day. So I make every effort to keep my feet safe

I sensed that there had to be something to believing in God though because I came to know a few people from our church and things were so different at their homes. There was prayer at dinnertime, smiles, hugs, laughter, and more. They would comfort and encourage each other. Lift up and build instead of beat down and discourage. They even did it for me. They made me feel loved, smart, and valuable. I often wished I could run away and live with some of these families.

As I got older, between five and seven, I loved to play in the big lot off of our property. I would venture off with Jared, Sara, and a few neighborhood kids and stay out until we were called in. This is my best childhood memory. We would play house, the way it was supposed to be. I knew when I grew up, that was how it would be. I would live to make my children happy. My husband and I would be loving and kind to each other all the time.

My mother had terrible mood swings. I didn't know until I was around twelve years old or so that it was due to alcohol and that not all people drank.

My father had the same problem, although he became happy, social, and calm, which I think only made my mother angrier for some reason. It was as if she didn't like seeing him happy or anyone else for that matter.

From time to time my parents would attend and have family gatherings. They were fun for the kids and for the adults. My father's family didn't like my mother much. There was a lot of negative, hateful gossip in his family about her, which my mother returned.

As I got older, I think I realized that the best thing to be in my home was invisible.

I did have occasional visits to my grandparents' house. For some reason they were really excited to have me for a couple of months in the summer while I was out of school. It was my grandfather who especially made me feel special. I only spent the summer with them a few times because when I was around nine, I didn't want to come back home and cried for days when I returned.

My mother decided to beat the sadness out of me. She also told me it was the last time I would stay with my grandparents, and it was. I mean truly who would want to return to a place where it seemed like you could do nothing right after you spent two months in a place where it seemed you could do no wrong?

Like I said, it seemed like in those days happiness was not allowed. So we would try not to show it, at least not to her.

I do remember that I loved to roller-skate, go swimming at the local pool, and play after-school games.

Junior high school was all right. I liked going to different classes and seeing different people, although I wasn't very social. I was more of an observer. I didn't participate in any of the extracurricular activities because I was afraid to ask my mother if I could.

I do remember that I loved to ride bikes and play with my girlfriend next door. Her name was Sandra.

She was a very nice Christian girl from a very nice Christian family. She invited me to go to her church with her family once in a while. She moved to Texas just before we were about to enter the eighth grade. We wrote to each other for a while but lost touch.

To tell you the truth, I don't remember much about my junior high school years. They were kind of like living in a pit, kind of just living to survive. I couldn't wait to grow up and make a life of my own.

My parents didn't attend my graduation since it was just junior high. I didn't understand why everyone else's families were making such a big deal of it at the time.

Not much I know, but that's it and just in time. You're up.

Chapter 4

First Memory to Junior High—Mason

Wow! That went by fast.

Okay, here I go. I was born Mason Thomas Scott.

My first memory is my mother singing "You Are My Sunshine" to me when I was around three or four years old.

My mother was very sweet and delicate. Nothing ever seemed to bother her. She always had a defense for a rude, unkind person and loved the Lord so very much.

She smiled almost all the time.

"Mason, sweetie, come here. Do you want to help Mommy make some cupcakes?" my mother asked me as she had so many times before.

"Yeah, yeah!" I screamed.

I loved baking and doing crafts with my mom. She was so absolutely loving. We would do this from time to time until I was almost ten.

My mom, dad, and I would attend church every Sunday. Mom never missed and made sure Dad and I would always accompany her. She didn't force my dad to go. She just faithfully made it a routine that my father seemed to have no problem with.

I remember my dad would play outside with me from time to time. He would chase me around the yard and throw me in the air so high I thought I might touch the sky. We had so much fun. I really loved him. I did my best to ignore things that didn't seem right just like my mother did.

Although my dad attended church routinely, he always complained. If it wasn't this, it was that. No one could do anything right there it seemed. My mom would remind him that most of the ushers and people who helped out at church were volunteers. It didn't help.

My dad worked in the local steel plant. He often would get home late because he would go out with some of his work friends and drink.

My dad was a very unpredictable person. He could be the nicest, friendliest person one minute but turn on a dime because of something you said or something he would just think of.

As I got older, I would help him with the yard work and with washing the car. I never did anything right in his eyes. It got worse as I got older.

Dad would say, "I can't believe how stupid and lazy you are. I can't believe God gave me such an idiot for a son. I must have really done something to make him really mad."

I was around seven, and I would just cry and ask God to make me a better son so I could make my daddy happy. I wanted to be a good son just like Jesus was to God.

I would hear my mother softly telling my dad to please not treat me like that.

"You're his father, and he loves you," my mom said. "He wants to please you, Phillip. You need to teach him and encourage him to be a good man."

She would tell him this all the time.

At first when she tried to defend me, he would just tell her to shut up or simply put up his hand to wave her off and ignore her.

I remember the first time I heard him slap her when she came to my defense. I ran so fast into the kitchen where they were talking.

At only eight years old I bravely screamed at my dad, "You leave her alone!"

He laughed and said, "What are you going to do, you little piece of nothing," as he kicked me into the wall.

My mother screamed and ran up to me. My dad just laughed and left.

I told my mother I would be a better son so that Dad would not be mean to her. My mom said I was a wonderful son. I was her sunshine and would always be.

She told me that when I came into the kitchen that day, I was like a little David intent on protecting her from Goliath. She said she loved me for my bravery but to never do that again and to be respectful to my father.

Mom and I learned to just let things go and act like things like this never happened.

Mom said, "Good Christians forgive just like God forgives us. We just need to pray for him, Mason."

When my dad had his hateful episodes, he would also act like they never happened and be good until the next time … and so on and so on.

After acting awful, he would just come in and start acting like nothing happened, and if someone looked upset, he would just get mad again, so we always tried to look happy even if we were still hurt from his actions.

Truly I was afraid of my dad. I prayed and prayed for him to love me and did everything to try to please him. It truly hurt when he and I would have our good days, and I would fall in so much love with my daddy, my precious father. Then all of a sudden he would turn on me, and I was nothing again. I never truly knew where I stood with him. It made me a very nervous kid.

After school one day I ran home and started cleaning up the yard. I began immediately pulling weeds, raking the million or so pine needles off our lawn, and then watering it. I tried to do it just like dad did. I just knew my dad would be so proud.

When he got home that night, I couldn't wait to surprise him. Dad immediately looked around the yard and then went straight to the garage.

I ran in after him and said, "Hi, Dad, did you see what I did all by myself just like you taught me?" I was still sweaty and dirty from all my hard work but so happy.

Dad said, "Am I supposed to be happy? Don't start something you can't finish and expect me to come home after working all day and pick up after you. If you are too stupid to do it right and put everything back where it belongs, don't do it at all."

I was crushed, but I didn't want my mom to see, so I ran off and had a good cry. I didn't want her to confront my dad.

When my dad was angry, he had a very scary dark look in his eyes. It was like he became someone else. That was the person I did not like. I'm afraid to say, but that was the person I hated.

One day Mom and I spent the afternoon doing crafts and making cupcakes for the church fundraiser the next day.

This was surely going to be the best day of my life in a long time. I was going to be nine in two weeks, and I planned on joining the Pop Warner football team. I just knew my dad would be proud. He loved football.

My dad got home a little earlier than expected that day. Mom was running a little behind on dinner. I was in the kitchen with my mom.

Mom and I could read my dad so easily.

As he walked up to the front porch of our old Victorian house, his body language and look on his face was fair warning to stay quiet and keep your distance.

My dad started on my mom right away.

"Is dinner ready?" he asked my mom hatefully.

Mom sweetly smiled and said, "Just a few more minutes, honey. It will be ready almost as soon as you get settled."

He looked at me and said, "Why are you always under your mother's feet! You act like a little sissy girl. What kind of son are you?"

"I was helping Mom make cupcakes for church" I replied sheepishly.

"Oh, you were helping Mommy make cupcakes for church", he mocked me. "These stupid-looking things right here?" he asked me.

I just nodded my head.

He looked at me with such anger and hatred. I thought I would never know why. He picked up the tray and pushed it into my face. There went all the cupcakes. He grabbed me by my arm and threw me to the ground and started toward me.

Oh, I forgot to mention he was an alcoholic, a real mean drunk.

Anyway, the next thing that happened was truly amazing. I could not believe my eyes!

My mother, that sweet, sweet, godly woman, clobbered my dad with a skillet. She knocked him out cold!

My mom called the police and our pastor. The police arrested my dad.

Our pastor went to the jail to talk to my dad. He tried to counsel him on his inappropriate behavior and to inform him that my mother was seeking protection from the church. He told my dad that he would like to begin a weekly counseling session with the family when he was released.

Dad was insulted and embarrassed. He became very angry and told the pastor that it was none of his business. He would fix things himself when he got home. He would teach us both some godly respect, and he didn't need his help to do it.

The pastor took that as a threat and advised my mother to stay with a friend for a couple of days.

Mom and I packed a few things and went to stay with James and Emily Paulson. They were a very nice couple that attended our church. Emily and my mom were very close friends for more than five years. Mr. Paulson tried to bond with my dad, but Dad brushed him off. Dad had his own kind of friends and wanted nothing to do with Mr. Paulson.

The Paulsons did not have any children. They tried for many years to have them and even tried to adopt, but things never worked out for them. They latched on to me quickly. I loved being around them whenever possible. They were awesome and loving to all the children at our church, but for some reason they took especially to me.

The Paulsons were waiting eagerly at the door when we arrived. Mom and I felt so welcomed. After Mom and I settled in our room, we went back downstairs. Mom and Miss Emily went straight into the kitchen to start making dinner. I could hear my mom crying.

Mr. James sensed my sadness and concern. He patted my head and said, "So what do you say to a game of checkers, young man?"

"Sure," I said.

The whole incident enraged my dad. The fact that my mom had the nerve to bring strangers into our personal business totally drove him off the deep end.

When he was released from jail, he went to the house and broke everything he could. He put countless holes in the walls and left. That was the last time I saw my dad.

He left my mother and me with nothing. Our house was a rental, and the landlord was very upset with the damage. My mother could not afford to continue renting it. My dad cleaned out the bank account and left town. We salvaged what we could.

The Paulsons were truly God's gift to us. They told my mother she and I could live with them until she got on her feet.

It broke my heart to see my mother so broken. There was nothing I could do to help her. I felt so useless.

Things settled down quickly for Mom and me soon after dad left. Mom found a job at a local restaurant a couple of blocks from the Paulsons' antique shop. Mom loved working in the diner and doing volunteer work for our church. She truly blossomed with her newfound freedom.

She was no longer fearful of doing what made her happy. She was free to be herself.

Mom also helped the Paulsons in their antique shop by doing various task. They would travel to Europe once a year and make quarterly trips to other places to search out antiques and other unique furnishings.

Mom and I would manage things while they were gone. They invited me on a few trips, but I would not leave my mom's side for a second.

I loved living with the Paulsons. We had great family dinners together. We talked about the Lord and how great and wonderful he is. Life was looking up.

I was excited about starting junior high. A few years had passed since we had moved in with the Paulsons. The Paulsons insisted we stay with them.

Mom and I went shopping for school clothes and some school supplies. I admired her so much. She was such a great example of a Christian woman. Actually she was a great example of a great Christian—period. I felt like the luckiest kid in the world to be her son. Because of this, I told myself that I was going to make her so proud. I was going to become the best man I could possibly be. I would take such good care of her when I grew up. I had such plans.

I would tell her all the time that I would buy her the best of everything when I got older. I would work hard and make lots of money.

Mom would just smile and say, "Oh, Mason, God made me the richest person in the world when he gave me you."

One afternoon I was cleaning the counters in the antique shop when Mr. Porter, the manager of the restaurant where my mother worked, came running in. He anxiously said, "Mason, come quick. Your mother is ill."

Uncle James quickly ran over to me and said, "Let's go."

We ran the two blocks to the restaurant. I could hear the sirens of the approaching emergency vehicles in the distance.

As I ran through the front door, I was guided to the back room. They had taken my mother to a back office and laid her on the sofa.

I grabbed her hand and cried, "Mom, Mom—" She squeezed my hand and held it tight. Her eyes opened slightly, and she smiled to the best of her ability. I felt her hand go limp, and then she passed away. Just like that, she was gone. Just like that.

I cried out, "No. Mom! No. Momma. Mommy, please wake up! Please, please don't leave me. I love you. I love you— God! Please help her. Help my mom." I held her so tight until they pulled me away.

They said it was an aneurysm that took her.

I'm sorry Cynthia, I think I went way over my allotted time period.

Cynthia was absolutely speechless. She was so afraid she would cry. They just looked at each other for a while and laughed at the awkwardness.

Finally she said, "Oh Mason! That was so absolutely heartbreaking. I am so glad you had such a loving, wonderful mother. I know I've only known you a few hours, but it shows in your character. Your mother is still with you, you know. I am so sorry for how your dad treated you, but how lucky you were to have such an amazing mother, even for such a short time. I find it so amazing how people who are supposed to love us can be so hateful? How wonderful and amazing God is that he teaches us how to forgive. How wonderful and amazing he forgives us as well."

Mason said, "Well, you didn't have such a good time either, and you seem to have turned out pretty well. Forgiveness truly does help us to become better people. I am sure of it. I'm anxious to hear the next two chapters of your story. Are you still okay with it?"

"Sure, if you are," she replied. "And you didn't quite make it through junior high school, so you will have to continue please," she told Mason.

"Are you sure?" Mason asked. "I don't want to take up all of our time telling my story and leave you short of time. I want to hear your story too, all of it."

"I will have plenty of time," Cynthia said to Mason.

Cynthia just had to step away for a few minutes to get a hold of her emotions. She was so taken by Mason's story.

"Before you get started again Mason, I'm going to have to ask you to excuse me for a restroom break before you continue. Is that okay?" Cynthia said.

"Of course, no problem," Mason replied as he got up from his seat and let her out of the row.

Cynthia barely made it to the restroom before the tears started to run down her face. She was so upset at the story about Mason's mother. She began to sob softly. Deep down she knew it wasn't only Mason's story, but it was also her story.

She felt so guilty for feeling bitter and envious when Mason first started his story. She barely kept from rolling her eyes when she felt it was leading to a perfect life, while she had just shared her pathetic life with him. She prayed that he did not notice. All she could do now was ask God to forgive her.

Remembering her past and seeing her life in parts of Mason's story overwhelmed her. She knew she needed to get a hold of herself before she went back to her seat. She felt so silly. She began to pray for strength and comfort.

When she felt like she looked convincingly together, she headed back to her seat. She had been in the restroom for quite a while and didn't want to cause any concern.

Mason hoped he didn't upset her with his story. She seemed surprisingly sad. He had almost convinced himself that he hadn't upset her, but when Cynthia returned to her seat, he knew he had.

He would act like he didn't notice that she had been crying. He would show no emotion one way or another. He learned that from living with his dad.

Before Mason began his story from where he had left off, he gentlemanly asked Cynthia, "Are you sure you want to continue this." He was so amazed at her strength in her story; however, he was sensitive to the fact that it was still somewhat emotionally draining. And he knew his story was headed toward a very low point for him, and he remembered that it left her in tears. He loved her for that.

What did he just say to himself? He loved her? He dismissed the thought immediately.

Cynthia quickly replied, "Oh, yes, Mason, of course I want you to proceed. I am anxious for you to continue from where you left off. Plus we made a deal."

"Okay, here I go," he said.

Uncle James took me home. As much as he tried, my poor uncle James could not hold back his tears. He told me over and over again that he was so sorry. As if he could do something about it. I was numb, just sobbing.

As soon as we drove up to the house, I jumped out of the car and ran to my mother's room. I climbed on her bed and laid down on it. I thought that I would stay there forever … until I died and would be with my precious mother again.

The Paulsons tried so hard to comfort me. I think back now how difficult my mother's death was to them as well. They both loved her so much. Like a daughter. They stayed so strong for me.

They kept coming into the room and checking on me every so often. When twenty-four hours passed and all they could get me to do was drink water, they knew they had to do something. I wasn't eating anything. I wasn't speaking at all. Nothing mattered now, I thought. It was all over. I wasn't going to grow up to make my mother happy and give her everything she ever wanted. She was my purpose for living, for breathing. My mom was gone forever. Why did God do this to her, such a loyal, loving person! Why did God do this to me? I was so mad at him, so confused.

Two days after my mother passed, Uncle James came into my mother's room for the hundredth time or so where I was still lying motionless. He was determined to get me up and out of the room.

He said, "Mason, I know none of this makes sense to you, son. But your mom left you a legacy. Your mother would not want to see you so broken and hurt. She believed in God with all of her heart, and you know that, son. She lived her life in a way where she knew that one day she would be with God in heaven. I believe and you should too, without any doubt whatsoever, that that is where she is right now.

"Now I know we would rather have her here with us. But you have to believe, son, she is in a better place right now. Your mother believed that God knew what he was doing, and even though it doesn't make any sense right now, we need to be strong and believe that too … in your mother's honor.

"Now tomorrow we are going to lay your mother to rest. Because of the wonderful woman she was, a lot of people have contributed to her funeral expenses and the celebration of her life.

"As her son, the treasure of her life, Mason, you should be there, my boy, and stand up like David against the giant that wants to keep you locked up in this room and crush your mother's dreams.

"Your mother gave you a life to live, and she praised God for you every day. She would want you to live your life to the fullest. Can you do that for her, Mason?"

I knew how hard it was for my uncles James to have that talk with me without shedding a tear. That wonderful man gave me the strength I needed to get up. I sat up on the bed, looked into my uncle's eyes, and said, "Yes." I wrapped my arms around his neck and began to sob. He held me so tightly until I stopped.

We both went downstairs together. Aunt Emily gave me an even bigger hug and kiss. We all sat down for lunch.

The next morning we attend my mother's funeral and celebration of life. The program had a picture of my mother with her full name—Estelle Louise Mason Scott. My mother was the only child of very elderly parents. They died shortly after I was born. I was named Mason to honor my grandparents. My middle name, Thomas, also came from my grandfather as well as my dad.

My grandfather's full name was Graham Thomas Mason. My grandmother's full name was Francis

Louise Mason. My maternal grandfather and dad actually got along very well, my mother used to tell me. When I was born, my dad was more than happy to honor my grandparents with my name. Thomas was my father's middle name, so we pretty much had the whole family covered with my name.

Anyway, I got through the service okay, and I started junior high a few weeks later. The Paulsons became my legal guardians. They tried to locate my father to show legal steps were taken to contact him. Later my uncle would say that he and Aunt Emily really didn't try very hard to find my dad because they loved me so much and wanted to keep me all to themselves.

Uncle James and Aunt Emily were nothing less than angels in my life. They were so loving, nurturing, and kind. I knew how very blessed I was to have them in my life. They treated me like a son, and they are everything to me.

Junior high school went by very quickly. The Paulsons kept me very busy. Although I would never stop missing my mother, keeping busy helped tremendously to deal with her passing.

During this time Uncle James taught me truly what a father was. He wasn't afraid to tell me he loved me and that he was proud of me. He bragged about me to everyone who would kindly listen.

I did everything I could to give him as much material as possible. I did well in baseball, got good grades, and helped around the shop. Uncle James built up my self-esteem and confidence.

Aunt Emily equally loved me. She took the place of my mom, but she did it very subtly. She was careful so that I didn't feel she was trying to take my mother's place and offend my mom's memory. I grew to love them both very much.

I sometimes wonder how different I would be without these wonderful people in my life. I could have easily been filled with resentment and bitterness. God is truly good.

Anyway, I stayed after school a lot for baseball practice and spent a lot of time with my best friend, Pete. We would race our bicycles at a nearby field with a bunch of other kids whenever we had some free time. We spent a lot of time out there.

Pete had a little sister named Lilly. She was around three years younger than us. She was a grade school kid, and we were almost in high school and couldn't be bothered by her. Actually she was a bit of a pest. Pete use to tease me and say that his sister liked me.

"Yeah, right. She's just a kid," I would say.

"Well, that's it, Cynthia. I'm finally finished! First memory through junior high."

Chapter 5

Plane Talk

The attendants were already in the middle of their second beverage service.

"This little testimony challenge is getting very interesting Mason. That was a great story. I can't wait to hear the rest of it."

"You should get started with part two of your story as soon as we finish our beverages."

"I sure will," agreed Cynthia.

"Would you like something to drink?" the attendant asked Cynthia.

"Yes, please. I will have coffee with cream and sugar."

As the attendant handed Cynthia her coffee she asked Mason, "And for you sir?"

"I'll have the same, thank you."

The attendant handed Mason his coffee.

"I am so anxious to hear more Cynthia. I'm still feeling a little guilty for being so long-winded on my first part. I just can't believe how the words just spilled out of me."

"I told you it would be like therapy."

It seemed like the activity on the plane had really calmed down. It was very quiet, and a lot of people were sleeping. They would have to keep their voices down, or everyone was going to hear their stories. They also did not want to disturb anyone's sleep.

Cynthia reached into her briefcase and took out her box of circus animal cookies and said to Mason, "Would you like some?"

Mason smiled at her and her little box of cookies and said, "Sure I'll have a couple. Thanks." *How cute is that.*

"So where exactly are you headed?" Mason asked as he sipped his coffee.

"I'm off to Milan for business," Cynthia replied. "I'm a buyer's assistant for a small designer store chain. I will be there until the end of the week. Well, Thursday anyway." Cynthia continued, "And where is your final destination? London?"

"Heaven, I hope," he said and smiled cutely. "Okay, that was actually a little corny." They both laughed.

"I'm headed for Rome for a couple of days. I visit various places to find interesting pieces for my aunt and uncle's antique shop."

"Oh, for Aunt Emily and Uncle James, right?" she replied quickly and knowingly. She was surprised at how proud she felt for knowing this.

Mason smiled and said, "Yes, for Aunt Emily and Uncle James." *How absolutely adorable she is*, he thought.

"And then I am off to Paris for a day," Mason continued.

"That sounds so exciting. You must absolutely love your job," Cynthia added.

"Yes, I do in fact, but it gets a little lonely sometimes. My wife went on one of my trips once before she got sick. We went to France and Spain. She loved it. It was fun to have someone to enjoy the sights and the whole experience of traveling to Europe," Mason explained. "I was just thinking earlier that I would like to bring my son, Tom, on one of my trips. Somehow we've never made it to Europe. He traveled with my wife and me to Hawaii and Australia, but those trips were just for vacation," Mason continued.

"Bryce has never been outside of California, other than when we visited the Grand Canyon and went to Las Vegas. We also went to a baseball tournament in Phoenix. He received a small scholarship for college in northern California," Cynthia remarked. "He would have loved to go to college out of state. He was hoping for Colorado."

"As for me, if I didn't have this job I would never have seen anything else but California, Nevada, and Arizona as well. It may not show, but I am not much of a traveler anyway. I really don't care for it. It could be because, just like you, I don't have anyone to enjoy it with. If I could bring Bryce, I'm sure we would have a blast," Cynthia continued.

Cynthia finished her coffee and put her trash inside the empty box of animal cookies. She turned to Mason and said, "You know I rarely share my favorite cookies with anyone."

"I'm honored to be a recipient of this rare yet kind gesture, dear lady," Mason replied with a playful serious look and slight bow.

"As you should be kind sir'" Cynthia replied dramatically.

The flight attendant quickly collected their trash and proceeded down the aisle.

"Well, Cynthia, we are now almost eight hours into our flight, so we'd better continue our stories if we want to be able to finish. Please take as much time as you need. I have already taken more time than I should have," Mason said with a guilty smile.

Chapter 6

High School to College— Cynthia

Okay, here I go. In high school I was still somewhat of a recluse.

I had already convinced myself that invisible was the best way to be. I sat back and watched people who seemed to have it all together, happy and carefree young adults.

I saw girls hanging out together in various groups and guys doing the same thing. You had the cool kind of kids and the quiet groups that were just glad to have someone to hang out with. Everyone seemed happy and content with their lives.

There were a few bullies and troublemakers. I always felt how awful it was for someone to think hurting another person was fun. I did my best to stay away from these types, but somehow they would find a way to get to you.

It really wasn't until my senior year that I grouped up with some girls from my physical education class. We planned to skip school one day. Shows what we knew. Who is not going to figure out that we were all together? We were on the same squad.

Well, we did get caught, but we were just warned thankfully. This was the highlight of my high school years, a rebel for a day.

None of the girls in my group went to our senior prom. Looking back, I think we were all just a bunch of misfits, but we were glad to have had each other. I did have fun with them. We did go to our graduation night celebration and had a pretty good time.

We were not really close friends. None of us stayed in touch. I barely remember their names. Not much to my high school days either I'm afraid.

It's not that I would not have liked to have had friends in school. It's that I was kind of embarrassed of my family. The thought of even having a boyfriend of any kind was out of the question. My mother would have killed me. She made everything so nasty and dirty. I didn't know until later what the reason was for her acting like this.

I did have a little crush on one of the football players, but that was about it. It was a very far-fetched fantasy. It was kind of like *Beauty and the Beast*, me being the beast. Of course, I never managed to speak more than three words to this person. I was really pathetic and overweight, and I didn't know a thing about makeup or hair. This made me enormously self-conscious and shy.

By the time I got to college, I was a little more open and less withdrawn. I was asked out on a few dates but made excuses for not being able to go. I had zero confidence. And according to my mother, they only wanted one thing, and it sounded pretty scary.

My sister, Sara, got married to a very nice guy. She met him in college. After he graduated, he got a job as a dental assistant, and a few years later he became a dentist and started his own practice.

Of course my mother didn't like Brian and made it a little hard for Sara at first. As soon as my mother realized that Sara could care less what she thought and that Sara was going to marry him no matter what she thought, her attitude changed.

I was so glad for my sister. She was really a great example of a good person to me. I really love her.

Seeing my sister so happy helped me realize that maybe men were not as evil as my mother made them seem. I had also seen enough romantic movies and read several romance novels that convinced me that being in love with a man did not sound scary at all.

I first met my soon-to-be husband in January of my junior year in college. About that time I was so afraid that I would be alone all my life. I was completely swept off my feet at how attentive he was to me. He would tell me I was pretty and thought everything I had to say was important.

Of course, I took extra care of myself to dress nicely and even lost some weight. I felt so wanted and loved. It was the best feeling I ever felt. I was so in love.

I met him at my cousin's wedding. He was a police officer. His name was Jack Stuart. He was three years older than me. My parents seemed to like him. He was always a gentlemen and helpful.

He loved to talk with my dad. He was always respectful to my parents. We dated for about a year and a half and got married two weeks after I graduated from college. I was on top of the world. I just knew that my life was going to finally be all that I wanted it to be. I was so absolutely sure. Loneliness had surely departed from my life forever. Life was good.

So there you are, Mason, high school to college in a nutshell.

Chapter 7

High School to College—Mason

Well, about three years into high school here comes Miss Lillian Rose Baxter, looking as cute as ever in her new big-girl, high school clothes.

"Wow … just wow," I said louder than I thought.

I just stood there frozen with my eyes fixed on her. All of a sudden I heard Pete cracking up at me as he smacked me on the back of the head.

"Jeez, snap out of it, man!"

Not long after that I did everything possible to be near Lilly. Volunteered at school, church, and wherever else I knew she would be.

Neither Lilly nor I were allowed to date. Uncle James said, "When you know where your life is going and how you plan on supporting yourself let alone a potential bride, then you can think about it."

I had every intention of doing just that.

After I graduated from high school, I ended up applying for and being accepted at San Diego State

College, which wasn't too far from home. I did stay at the dorm but saw my aunt and uncle at least twice a month.

San Diego to my home near Ontario, California, which is located in what they call the Inland Empire, was about two hours by car. It was a pretty easy drive both ways.

I was very excited about attending college. I majored in business management with a minor in communications. I knew without a doubt that my mother would be so proud. I could imagine her sweet, loving smile. I loved her so much and still missed her immensely.

I would come home at holidays, on special occasions, and for the summer as well.

I will have to confess that Lilly was the first one I looked for when I got home. Both our folks made sure we were not left alone for too long. And even with their careful, watchful eyes, Lilly and I found a way to have some time together and steal a little smooch or two here and there.

We were surely rebels.

Lilly ended up going to a local college for nursing. There was no way she was going to get to attend a college near me. Our parents didn't trust us for some reason.

I was now a sophomore and working part-time at a small company in San Diego, and I hoped to do my internship there. I thought it would be a good time to ask Lilly to marry me after I graduated and found a more permanent job. I would be around twenty-one, and she would be nineteen or so and still attending college.

Early in my senior year I received a call from the administration office. They informed me that a relative of my father was trying to get a hold of me. The office would not share any information with this person; however, they advised the woman that they would give me her contact information.

My stomach knotted up instantly, and my heart began to race. Why was she looking for me? I immediately called my uncle and told him what happened.

"Call her, Mason," said Uncle James. "That is the only way you will find out why she is looking for you. And don't worry, Mason. You are a little too old for them to take you away from us."

I called her the next day as Uncle James suggested.

"Hello," said the voice on the other end of the line.

"Hello, my name is Mason Scott. I was informed that you were trying to locate me."

"Oh, yes, Mason, thank you for calling. My name is Margaret Taylor. I'm your father's sister, your Aunt Margaret," she continued.

"I'm sorry, but I haven't seen my father since I was ten, which is more than ten years ago. I really don't know much about him, so I don't know how much I can help you," I replied.

"Well, the reason I'm calling Mason is that I really would like to meet you, and so would your grandfather. Unfortunately he is very ill and is not expected to live much longer. If you would be so kind to agree to meet us, we can arrange transportation."

"Where is it that you live?" I asked.

"In Santa Barbara," Margaret replied.

"I'm going to have to check my schedule to see when I might be able to come. Also, my uncle is going to want to come with me. Would that be okay? He's kind of over protective," I said.

"Sure, that is not a problem at all," Margaret replied. She gave me the address, and I told her I would call back and let her know what day I could drive down.

When I called my newfound aunt to let her know I could come down this coming weekend, she was very excited. She said that perhaps we could talk a bit before I came up to fill me in on my father's life as a child as well as the relationship between my father and grandfather. She said she didn't want me to be surprised about things her father might say.

I called my aunt Margaret on Friday, the day before my visit to confirm that my uncle and I would arrive around 11:30 a.m. She was very pleased and informed me that she would have some lunch prepared for our meeting.

My aunt began telling me about my father's life. She was his older sister. She said my father was extremely close to his mother, my grandmother. Their father, my grandfather, was very busy with working and traveling for his company.

My dad's mother would get them to football and ballet practice. She was amazing. She said that her father was never really loving or attentive to them but that he did provide for them very well. They had the best of everything. His relationship with them was more like a business or obligation.

"When Phillip was in elementary school, he did everything he could to get our father's positive attention. By junior high he gave up. The good thing was that Mom did her best to try to make up for our father's absence and lack of interest," Margaret continued.

"Mom would run herself ragged sometimes. My dad hated it, but she was always the one everyone depended on to make all occasions perfect.

"One day while she was getting ready for Phillip's football game, she ran into the kitchen to gather all the treats she had baked and some drinks she had bought for a luncheon they were holding after the game. She tripped over a rug and hit her head on the corner of the counter. She died instantly. This ripped Phillip apart and seemed to build an even greater divide between him and our father," Margaret explained to me and Uncle James.

After my aunt and I spoke, I thought that perhaps that was the reason my dad would get so angry when I was helping my mother bake as a little boy. Perhaps it brought back the terrible memory of his precious mother's death. And I definitely know the heart-wrenching feeling of losing a precious mother.

I was very grateful and touched by my aunt's story.

On Saturday morning my uncle and I arrived in Santa Barbara and drove up a very long driveway. The house looked like a museum. It looked really cold. I thought this must be a hospice care facility or ritzy convalescent hospital.

As we approached the front door, my aunt came out to greet us. I was amazed at the resemblance to my father.

My aunt led us into a large room that had some appetizers and drinks set out. We sat down for a while and talked casually about our trip and the weather.

"Well, Mason, are you ready to meet your grandfather?" she asked me.

"Sure," I replied, trying to sound confident.

My grandfather was sitting up in his bed. He was eighty-seven years old and looked very weak. I was told he had a bad heart condition and could go anytime.

My newfound aunt Margaret walked just ahead of me and said to her father, "Dad, this is Mason, Phillip's son."

"Hello, Mason," he said. "It is nice to finally meet my grandson."

"Nice to meet you, sir," I replied and extended my hand.

"You have a strong handshake there," my grandfather complimented. I just smiled.

"As you know, I am not doing well, and a man tends to think at times like these who's going to carry on his name. And here you are. Mason Thomas Scott, right?"

"Yes, sir," I replied.

"A very nice strong name," my grandfather continued.

"Thank you," I responded again with a smile.

"Well, I know where Thomas and Scott came from, but where did Mason come from?" my grandfather asked.

"It was my mother's family name," I answered.

"You know if your parents named you Phillip Thomas Scott, you would have been the third. Phillip Thomas Scott the third," my grandfather continued.

"No, sir, I didn't know that," I replied.

"I understand you were raised by your mother's brother after your mother passed," my grandfather said.

"No, sir, I was raised by a couple my mother and I lived with before she died. They became my guardians."

"I don't understand. How come nobody tried to contact your father or relatives?" my grandfather replied almost angrily.

"Well, sir, there were efforts made to contact my father; however, no one knew where he moved to. And respectfully, sir, he really didn't want me or my mother in the first place. The couple that raised me really took great care of me, and they still do."

"Well, it sounds like you didn't have such a good experience with your father. You know he passed away a few years ago," my grandfather explained.

"Yes, sir, Miss Margaret told me," I replied.

"That's your aunt Margaret, you know," his grandfather snapped. "Your family," he continued.

"Yes, sir," I replied. I realized that my grandfather wasn't feeling well and was probably a bit grumpy because of it.

"Do you see all of this, young man? This is what a lifetime of work gets you. I tried to tell that to your father, but he just wanted to fight me all the way. That's why he took off—to get back at me. He had no sense of family. He didn't go to college or do anything to make something of himself. He was fine until his mother died. Then he became weak and worthless. He started hanging out with the wrong crowd. Then one day he just left."

My grandfather just kept rambling on and on so negatively about my father. This was the first time that I really felt some compassion for my father. No wonder he was so bitter. If only he'd let my mom and I love him— We really wanted to so much.

My grandfather proceeded to say, "You're probably thinking that you are in for a pretty nice inheritance."

"No, sir, I am not thinking that at all. I am actually insulted that you would even suggest that," I said, very agitated. "I am here because Miss Margaret requested that I come and fulfill your request to meet me. I was told that you were ill and perhaps may pass soon. I am not here for anything else. If you are satisfied, we can end the visit here."

"You have a lot of spunk, kid, but you cannot tell me you don't want your inheritance. It's a lot of money. I don't believe you are not interested. You are trying to deceive me. That is what you are doing, or you are just being stupid!" my grandfather snapped.

I was infuriated. What gave him the right to talk to me like that? I did my best to let it pass, but I couldn't hold back.

"Sir, my God in heaven has taken care of me and provided for me all of my life. I am blessed and healthy, able to work and earn my way. There is no greater inheritance than what I have already received from God, my heavenly Father. As I sit here and listen to your hateful remarks about my earthly father, I can't help but feel that God is finally telling me the reason my father could not love me. It's because he could not get passed you not loving him. I say this with all of my heart, grandfather. I have a greater inheritance to share with you than you do with me. If you would like, I can pray with you, and you can accept Jesus as you Lord and Savior. He is so amazing that even though you have given this world almost all of your life, if you open your heart to him, he will receive you right now."

"That is nonsense, absolute nonsense! You are even more messed up than your stupid father!" my grandfather snapped angrily.

"God bless you, grandfather. If you change your mind, give me a call." I turned and left the room. I went downstairs to where my aunt and uncle were sitting. I did not want to upset my grandfather any further and cause him to pass.

I felt so sad and hurt. My heart was beating so hard it hurt. For a minute I felt like I was going to cry, but I silently prayed for God to give me strength, which he did. I felt better almost immediately.

As I entered the large study where my aunt and uncle were sitting, I said sadly, "I'm very sorry, Miss Margaret, but my visit did not go very well."

"Now you don't worry yourself about it, Mason. Your grandfather is not the easiest person to have a conversation with. Please sit with us for a while and have some lunch," my aunt replied.

My aunt Margaret was actually a very nice Christian woman. She said the Lord had helped her to tolerate her father and act according to how God expected her to act and not how her father made her feel. She had also tried to speak of Jesus to her father, who just would not have it. She told me that she had been blessed with nice words from her father from time to time, which she held on to in order to help her through the worse times.

She told me that my father was very sorry for the way he treated my mother and me. He had called her the night before he passed away and said that he wanted to change and be a better person.

"He wanted to find you and your mother and at least apologize for his bad behavior. He was not strong enough to visit Dad yet. But he wanted to accept Jesus as his Lord and Savior that night, and he did," my aunt Margaret finished happily.

I began to cry. Why do people wait so long to call on God? How lucky I was to have a mother who truly helped me understand God's love … and to also be adopted by people who believed as well. I was glad to know that I would see my father in heaven, and I knew my mother would be too.

Aunt Margaret hugged me and said, "Your father would be so proud of you. I know he always was. He just didn't know how to express it."

After we finished our lunch, Uncle James and I politely thanked my aunt Margaret for her hospitality. She hugged me tightly and said, "Call me anytime. I would like for you to meet my husband and your cousins."

"I would like that," I replied.

A few days later I received a call from my Aunt Margaret. She said that my grandfather would like to see me again. She said he told her to tell me he would like some of that inheritance I had offered him.

I was overjoyed at what my aunt just said. Could it really be that my grandfather and I would actually have a relationship? But most importantly, would my grandfather actually accept the Lord and have a relationship with Jesus?

I went back to visit my grandfather again. My grandfather did accept Jesus as his Lord and Savior. I was so happy and excited to introduce him to Jesus, to read the Bible to him, and to find all the stories in the Bible that I could share with him.

My grandfather and I would watch movie after movie on Bible teachings. I would tell him countless stories of people who found Jesus in their lowest of lows. My grandfather was so enchanted and uplifted about my enthusiasm and love for life and people.

I spent my entire spring break with my grandfather. My grandfather told me that he had never felt love for another human being like he did for me and my aunt Margaret. He wished he could have known me as a child. He confessed that he had made a lot of mistakes in his life and had many regrets.

He told me that he knew his son, Phillip, wanted his love so much and that he was so selfish not to give it to him. He was so glad to hear that my dad accepted the Lord before he died. This was the only thing that brought him peace—that he would see my father and his wife again soon.

My grandfather jokingly said, "Could you imagine their shock?"

It turned out my grandfather lived for seven months after we first met. This was seven months longer than anyone expected.

I was at my grandfather's side along with my aunt Margaret when he passed. My grandfather had the same smile my mother had on her face as he took his last breath on this earth.

My aunt Margaret and I vowed to stay in touch. I visit her a few times a year.

After Mason finished part two of his three-part testimony, Cynthia slapped him on his shoulder and said, "Mason, now you are going to have to let me out again."

Mason smiled and stood up. "Sorry."

Once again Cynthia made her way to the restroom to get a hold of her emotions.

Mason couldn't help but think how absolutely adorable she was. She was so sweet and sensitive. He really liked her more than he thought possible after knowing her for just hours.

Chapter 8

After College to Present Day—Cynthia

When Cynthia returned to her seat, she could see that Mason was anxious for her to begin her story.

Time was running out. There were only about two hours left. She was a little uncomfortable with sharing this part of her life, as it was where she had struggled and endured the most.

Mason was so open with his feelings in his story. She feared that she could not be as strong and open as Mason was during the difficult parts of her story.

"Are you ready for part three?" Mason asked anxiously.

"Yes," Cynthia answered reluctantly.

Mason sensed her uneasiness. He had to admit this whole storytelling event had taken a lot out of him, and he wanted to make sure she was all right.

"If it gets uncomfortable for you Cynthia, don't continue. I don't want you to get upset reliving things that have long since passed, the day before your business meetings," Mason advised.

Cynthia was so touched by his heartfelt concern for her. She felt like she'd known him for years, not just hours. How she wished her husband would have had a similar caring quality.

"I'll be fine. Thank you, Mason. And now for my third and final chapter," Cynthia said with a smile.

The first two years of our marriage went very well. We both worked hard to save money to buy our first home. We were so excited about getting settled and starting a family. We were both anxious to have a baby as soon as we bought a house.

Jack's parents lived in Colorado. They were an older couple and were already retired when we met. He didn't talk much about them, and I only met them once at our wedding. He talked a lot about his brother, Jeff, who passed away from lung cancer a few years before I met Jack.

Jack and his best friend, Dan, earned extra money painting houses on the side. He and Dan would spend a lot of time together on side jobs. It didn't take long before we had enough to buy a house.

We found a beautiful home in the suburbs, and ten months later we had a beautiful baby boy, Bryce Jeffrey Stuart.

Bryce was the center of our world for the next couple of years.

I took a couple of years off of work to stay at home with our son. In those two years I started to participate at the children events held at a local church. It gave Bryce an opportunity to meet and interact with other children. He really enjoyed it, and so did I.

Jack and I started to attend church. It had been a while for me, and Jack really wasn't too happy about it. He had a bad experience in Sunday school when he was a child. He said the teachers were very mean, hateful and abusive.

I advised Jack not to judge Christianity by how people act. Most of us are a work in progress. Being a Christian is living by the Word of God or at least doing our best to do so. It isn't easy for anyone. All God expects us to do is our best and to reach out to him for guidance.

I would share the Bible stories with him. I would tell him about Jesus and how loving he was. I was actually starting to understand what going to church and believing in God was all about. I knew then at twenty-three years of age that God had always been with me and would always be.

Unfortunately things kind of went downhill from here.

Jack got laid off from his job. We were actually pretty blessed since I had just found a new job locally, and he was going to get a pretty good severance package that would allow him some time to find a new job without causing us to struggle. I tried to keep things positive.

Jack and Dan, who also got laid off, ramped up their house-painting business, but Jack began to get depressed. He began snapping and drinking more than usual. It got worse when Dan found a job and couldn't help with the painting jobs any longer.

Because Dan could no longer help Jack, he had to finish a job he and Dan started together, on his own. He had to finish the trim on a two-story home. He finally finished it. But as he was stepping down the ladder, it shifted to the side, and Jack fell to the ground, breaking a rib and twisting his ankle severely. The owners rushed him to the hospital. He was bandaged up and given a prescription for painkillers. The doctor said he would be fine in a few months.

About a month later Bryce wasn't feeling well and kept crying so miserably. I kept trying to comfort him. I think he had a stomachache.

Jack came in to the room and shouted, "Shut up!" at the top of his voice.

Of course it scared Bryce, who began to cry even louder.

I said to Jack, "Don't yell at him like that."

Before I knew it, I was on the floor. To my surprise and shock, he had slapped me so hard.

Jack instantly began to cry and picked me and Bryce up, apologizing. "I am so sorry, honey. Please, I am so sorry," he said as he sobbed uncontrollably. He cried for days.

I said nothing to anyone and did my best to cover the bruise he left on my face. This surely would never happen again. I knew it wouldn't. I wanted to believe it with all my heart. I prayed and prayed. I knew God was with me. Things would get better.

Jack healed and finally found a job in Apple Valley. It was a long commute for him, but he was happy to be working again. He really loved being a police officer.

Although he was easier to live with, he never returned to the same Jack I had married. Somehow I began to sense that it had something to do with the relationship he had with his parents and his brother because he seemed haunted by something.

I often wondered why Jack's parents seemed to be so removed from him. They didn't seem to want anything to do with him or Bryce and me for that matter.

Jack's relationship with Bryce was very shallow. It was up and down. Neither Bryce nor I could ever tell when Jack was going to blow up. He hadn't been physically abusive for years, but he was so horribly hateful at times.

We felt so ridiculously controlled. We had to live and think just like him as if we didn't have any rights to our own thoughts or emotions. I tried to ignore my thoughts of how much I hated him and wished he would just go way. I would feel so guilty for thinking such thoughts while professing to be a Christian.

I could deal with how he treated me, but it was unbearable for me to see how he treated Bryce. I prayed and prayed that Bryce would not grow up to be as awful as his father. It killed me when Bryce would cry in such frustration over how helpless he felt for not being able to reason with or stand up to his father.

I was called things I would never call my worst enemy. I was belittled in private and was told to keep my mouth shut when other people would try to probe into my life.

The truth was he wanted to pretend to be this great guy, but he was so transparent. People could tell the kind of person he was. I would catch him talking every once in a while to people, making up things that weren't true. He was really a sick person. I was stuck with him and didn't have any idea how to get away. How could I get me and Bryce away from this ugly negative person safely?

He mocked God. He acted like he knew everything. He tried to tell me he was a believer, but just talking to him, you knew he wasn't. God knew he wasn't.

I would often cry out to God to please take him away from me, to set me free. These are the times I most questioned God's love for me. How could he love Bryce and me and allow this person to make our lives so miserable. I may have deserved this, but not my son.

I prayed for God to change Jack's heart, to heal him from whatever it was that was holding him from a relationship with the Lord and with us.

Cynthia stopped. It was as if she was back in that dark place again. She looked into Mason's eyes as if she was pleading for mercy.

"I really can't share much more with you, Mason, because it still upsets me so much," Cynthia said to Mason.

Mason could feel her anguish and wanted to take her in his arms and comfort her. How could he be so moved by this woman? Perhaps it was because her story was so very familiar.

"That's fine, Cynthia. Please don't feel like you have to share things you don't feel comfortable with. If you would like to stop, it is perfectly fine with me. Really," Mason said to Cynthia.

"I'm okay, it just got to me for a minute, but truly it does feel good to talk about it."

Jack became addicted to prescription drugs and drank a lot. I'm sure this was the reason for his personality change. He became much more unbearable to live with. Bryce was becoming angrier and angrier as he got older. He would cower to his father and do whatever he said.

Bryce would plead with me to leave his dad. He would cry and tell me how much he hated him. He hated that his father went to church and acted like a complete jerk all the time. He wished he was dead. He told me one time with so much anger that we would be better off if Jack would just die. He said, "You know we would, Mom. You know it!"

It broke my heart because I knew how much Bryce wanted to love his father and wanted so much for his father to love him back.

Then came the day Jack began to yell at me because Bryce had left some dirty dishes in the kitchen sink and didn't clean up his mess adequately.

"I don't know what this idiot, lazy kid's problem is. Can't he clean up his mess? Where is he?" Jack shouted angrily.

"I'll do it. Bryce was running late for baseball practice, and I told him to get going that I would clean up for him," I said to Jack.

"Move!" Jack said hatefully and pushed me out of the way. He began filling the sink with water to wash the dishes. He kept ranting and raving angrily, saying awful, terrible things.

I don't know why or where it came from, but I stood up to Jack. I could not take it any longer. I told Jack that I had had it with his abusive, nasty behavior and wanted a divorce.

He grabbed me by my neck and pushed me up against the wall and began calling me a stupid, ignorant ... well, you know. And his mouth did not stop with every nasty, degrading word you could think of. I couldn't breathe and began to cry. I tried to scream for help but couldn't.

All of a sudden my thirteen-year-old son came up from behind Jack and put him in a choke hold. With all Bryce had in him, he began squeezing his neck. Jack immediately released me and began squirming and kicking, trying to get loose. I quickly picked up the phone and called the police. I was so afraid of what Jack would do if he got free, but Bryce was not letting go. All of a sudden Jack stopped moving, and I screamed for Bryce to let go.

I began trying to pull him off his father. Bryce finally let go. Jack was out but still breathing. The police showed up very quickly.

By the time the police arrived, our neighbor already ran over to our house because he heard me screaming for Bryce to let go.

Jack had begun to regain consciousness, and our neighbor advised him to sit still. Bryce was in the living room, very shaken up by the whole experience.

Jack was taken to jail. I was advised to get a restraining order. Jack was ordered to go to anger management classes. A couple of men from our church tried to counsel him. He talked to them and said he would keep in touch, but he didn't. It wasn't until he realized that I had no intention of staying with him that he began getting counseling at our church.

Bryce and I stayed at my sister Sara's house until I figured out what to do.

I have to believe that Jack was on his way to recovery. He opened up about his relationship with his parents.

He said that his parents were not very attentive or loving. It was as if he and his brother were in the way. They provided for them but had no interest in getting them involved in sports or college or anything. He said it was as if he and Jeff only had each other.

His mother did seem to favor Jeff some—that is, she spoke more to him. Jack said he was considered the rebel. He said that perhaps he was just doing anything to liven up things or to get some type of attention even if it was for the wrong reasons.

Jack started drinking and smoking when he was fifteen. He smoked for years before he quit. When his brother got lung cancer, Jack felt his parents blamed him for it, even though they never openly said so. Jeff never touched a cigarette.

Jeff really suffered, and it hurt his parents so much. It hurt Jack, but of course, he had no one to talk to him about it.

Jack confessed that he speculated a lot about things that were quite possibly not true. For example, he thought that his parents hated him. But how would he know otherwise? His parents never talked to him.

Jack said, "How was I supposed to know whether they loved me or not? They never told me that they did."

This was the most open conversation Jack and I had in a very long time.

After three months of separation and two and a half months of therapy, counseling, and quitting the painkillers, Jack called and told me how very sorry he was. He told me I was the most important and most wonderful thing that had ever happened in his life. He loved both Bryce and I more than anything, and he would like it if he could have an opportunity to make up for all the heartache he caused.

That same night he also talked to Bryce and told him how much he loved him and that he should have told him that more often. He apologized for being a lousy father and asked for the opportunity to try again.

Bryce told his father that he loved him too and wanted to try again as well.

I had arranged for Bryce to get counseling. I'm glad I did because it gave him the strength and courage to forgive his father. And he did the best he could to hear his father out.

Truly I did love Jack. I wanted so much for us to be together. His words were so sincere. They melted my heart. I couldn't wait to hold him in my arms again and for him to hold me.

Jack had asked if he could come by the following Saturday and take us to dinner. Bryce and I both agreed. We were both looking forward to it. Jack challenged Bryce to a game of basketball. They kidded each other about how badly they would outscore each other. I hadn't seen Bryce so happy for such a long time.

Unfortunately Jack never made it. He was killed in a car accident on his way to our house.

Bryce was so confused. He was truly hoping that he and his father would finally have the relationship he always dreamed of. He was so looking forward to it.

He came to me, sobbing one day, saying how much he hated his dad at times, but he didn't mean it. He thought he did, but he didn't.

"I loved him Mom. I really did."

"I know you did, Bryce," I told him. "And you need to know that your dad knew it too. Believe me, Bryce, when I say that your father loved you more than anything. He told me so, but what is most important is that he told you."

"That was almost five years ago," Cynthia said to Mason. "Since then Bryce and I have spent a lot of time together going on outings with friends. I've been busy with work, and he with school. And so here I am."

After Cynthia finished, she was taken aback by the look on Mason's face. He seemed so involved in her story, anguished, stressed.

"Oh, Cynthia, that was so sad," Mason said. "Wow— Excuse me. Now I need a restroom break. Then I will continue with the last part of my story." Mason got up quickly and made his way to the restroom.

Mason was so overwhelmed by Cynthia's story. He was amazed at how much her story paralleled his story as a child. He was Bryce. He began to cry as he felt all the feelings he knew Bryce felt. He hoped to God that Bryce was truly all right with all that he had gone through.

He was surprised at how helpless and angry he became when she told the story of her last physical encounter with Jack. He wanted to jump into her story and rescue her, to comfort her.

Cynthia was the angel his mother had been—so strong, so caring, so loving. It took a very special person to live through such heartache and not be absorbed in bitterness.

Chapter 9

After College to Present Day—Mason

Okay, here it is my last and final chapter.

After my graduation, which my aunt Emily and uncle James made a very big deal over, I proposed to Lilly. We were married the following year.

My aunt Margaret was in attendance with her family at both my graduation and wedding. I have grown to love her so much. She continually shares the better side of my father with me, and I tell her about my mother.

Lilly and I got married in Santa Barbara at my grandfather's estate. My aunt Emily and aunt Margaret worked together with Lilly and her mother to put together a very beautiful wedding. I just had to show up, which was fine with me.

Lilly continued to go to college, while I worked at the company where I did my internship. Lilly transferred to San Diego State to finish her studies. We enjoyed living in San Diego. It was beautiful.

We did plan to move back to the Inland Empire after she graduated, as I wanted to be close to my aunt and uncle so I could help them with their business, which was becoming more and more successful.

About three months after we were married, Lilly became very ill. I had to take her to the hospital. That is when we found out that she was going to have our first child. We were so happy and excited. The doctor was very concerned at how ill Lilly was and kept her hospitalized for a couple of days. It turned out it was a severe case of morning sickness.

I couldn't wait to tell our families. We both decided to tell them at Thanksgiving since everyone was going to be at Lilly's parents.

We arrived at Lilly's parents early on Thanksgiving Day. We were so anxious to tell someone, but we both agreed on the right time. While we were all sitting down for our meal, we traditionally would state what we were most thankful for.

When it was my turn, I said, "I am thankful for the Lord's blessings, for family and good friends. But most of all I am thankful to be able to add to this family with my new wife and baby to be."

Before I could even finish, the cheers and screams of joy filled the room. We all jumped up and hugged and kissed one another. It was a very special moment for us all. I quickly called my aunt Margaret to share the news. She was equally overjoyed.

Phillip Thomas Scott III was born seven months later, the absolute joy of our lives.

As you know, he goes by Thomas.

Looking into his little face when he was born, I knew he just didn't look like a Phillip. It seemed like such a grown-up name, and he was so tiny. Without thinking, I said, "Well, hello, Tommy." And that is what we called him since.

Lilly and I were a great team as far as parenting went. I did as much as I could so she could finish her studies. Our families helped a lot. After she graduated and Tommy was a little close to two, she became pregnant with our second child.

Unfortunately in her fifth month she miscarried. As much as we tried for more children, she never became pregnant again. It turned out that Tommy would be our only child.

We had a great and loving marriage. We lived, laughed, and played as well as worked and served the Lord through various ministries together.

We traveled near and far and enjoyed raising our son. We were inseparable and each other's best friend. Tommy loved playing baseball. He played in the youth leagues and then in high school. We were members of the booster club and got involved in whatever we could to support Tommy.

Tommy was very close to his mother. When I would see them together, it reminded me so much of how my mother and I were. I did everything to encourage their bond. It was amazing.

We truly had a blessed life. No one could ask for more.

My uncle Jack's business began to grow, and we thought of opening up another shop in Westwood. I had a little money that my grandfather left me, and I decided to go into a partnership with my aunt and uncle.

We opened a store in Westwood. We thought this would be a great location, as a lot of our customers were traveling from west Los Angeles to our shop near San Bernardino to shop at our store. Word of mouth I guess.

Both Lilly and I decided that we wanted to continue to live just north of Ontario. Thomas grew up there, and we did not want to move him. I would commute to Westwood each day.

I manage the Westwood store and hired a couple of people to help me out. The Westwood store did amazingly well almost immediately.

About a little more than two years ago Lilly began to complain about feeling tired all the time. She was always feeling some kind of pain. I kept telling her to go get a checkup, yet she always put it off.

One morning in December Lilly was getting ready to take Tommy to his last day of school before Christmas break and looked in the mirror. Her eyes were very yellow. She called me immediately. She sounded scared and nervous. I told her I would come home immediately.

We both went to the doctor's office for tests. It turned out she had pancreatic cancer. They gave her three months to live, but she hung in there for nine months.

I was devastated at the news. I kept my heartache and fear from her as much as possible. How would I ever be able to go on without her? She was the absolute love of my life. I knew her since I was a kid. She was my best friend … my everything.

She stayed so strong for us. She counseled us and instructed us on the things we would need to do in her absence. She organized and planned her service and repass. She was absolutely amazing and so brave.

She only cried for our sadness and did everything to convince us to be happy for her because she was going home to God in heaven. She prayed with us and for us continually. She was my angel, and God just wanted her back.

As her condition worsened, she would sleep often. I would softly sing our wedding song to her to try to get her to wake up. It was "Just You and I" by Eddie Rabbit and Crystal Gayle. Sometimes she would wake up, and sometimes she would just smile in her sleep.

Lilly received hospice care at our house for the last three months of her life. On the day she died, I softly sang her our wedding song for the last time. "Just you and I, sharing our love together, and I know in time, we'll build the dreams we treasure. We'll be all right, just you and I—" I held and kissed her hand as she passed away.

In the nine months or so before her passing, we did everything possible to prepare Tommy for this devastating loss. He had just turned eighteen, and he was very overwhelmed by the news that she would be leaving us. His life was just truly beginning, and his precious mother would not be there to share it with him.

I knew his pain and did what I could. I turned to Uncle James for help. He helped me through the loss of my mother, which now seemed like so many years ago. I hoped he could help me with Tommy as well. I hoped he would possibly be able to help me again.

I felt so betrayed by God. Why was God taking away another special woman in my life? He took my mother, and now he was taking my wife, my son's mother. Why?

My wife suffered so much. Watching a once-vibrant person die slowly was unbearable.

Tommy and I were already living without our precious wife and mother. She was in the hospital most of the time, and when she came home, she was bedridden.

Looking back, I believe her loss was much more bearable than if she would have been taken from us suddenly. After nine months we were in a better place to let her go and accept her passing.

Tommy began to cry uncontrollably when his mother passed. He wrapped his arms around her and would not let go. I grabbed his shoulders and leaned close to him and whispered softly to him, "She's free now, Tommy. She's with God in heaven, son." I told him we would be okay, that she would forever be with us.

I called everyone to let them know that Lilly had passed. After the mortuary picked up Lilly, I went upstairs to check on Tommy. I sat next to him on his bed and told him of his mother's and my wedding song, "Just you and I". I told him that those were our words now. "We will be okay, just you and I."

After I left his room, I went into the garage, opened the door to my car, and put in the CD to play our song … over and over again. I wanted to remember our song, our dance, our wedding day. I needed to get as much of the hurt and anger out of me as possible if

I was going to make it another day, if I was going to be able to help Tommy.

Mason finished his story and realized that Cynthia was crying. He touched her arm softly and said, "I'm sorry. I didn't mean to upset you."

Cynthia shook her head and reached into her bag to get some tissue to wipe her tears.

"Oh, Mason, don't pay any attention to me. I'm just a big baby. How beautiful and sad your story is. You were and are such a great husband and father." She started tearing up again. "I'd better go to the restroom and get a hold of myself," Cynthia said.

Mason stood up to let her pass.

Chapter 10

Time to Sleep

By the time Cynthia returned to her seat, she noticed that Mason had dosed off. Neither she nor Mason had slept much, and both were very sleepy. She tapped Mason softly on the shoulder, and he immediately stood up.

"Well, we did it," Mason started. "We finished our life testimonies, and I have to say … absolutely amazing. What a great privilege to have the pleasure of learning so much about you," he finished.

"I feel the same privilege and honor as well," Cynthia replied, finishing with a very big yawn.

"I think both of us need a little break, and perhaps we should try to catch up on some sleep," Mason said.

"That sounds like another great plan," Cynthia said.

"Well, happy dreams," Mason said with a smile.

Both Cynthia and Mason positioned themselves in relatively comfortable positions to sleep a little. They both drifted off to sleep quickly.

Cynthia was the first to wake up after about an hour or so. She looked over at Mason.

He is so amazingly handsome, she thought. His tanned skin and dark hair really brought out his bluish green eyes. She could not help but notice that earlier.

He was sleeping so soundly. She was actually freezing. It was very cold in the airplane. Perhaps that is why she woke up so quickly. She covered her legs with the airplane blanket and put her jacket over her shoulders across her chest.

She noticed Mason's blanket had slipped to his lap. She didn't want his sleep to be interrupted by getting cold, so she pulled his blanket up over his shoulders as well. He continued sleeping soundly.

How she would love to take care of him, although it seemed he didn't need any help. If he was truly the man he described in his stories, he was a very amazing person. All she could think of was that she would so much like to know more about him, to get to know him better. She hadn't felt this way about anyone since her husband.

Cynthia settled back into her seat and once again fell asleep quickly.

Chapter 11

Last Hour of Flight

Both Cynthia and Mason once again were awakened by the clinking of dishes as the flight attendants prepared for the final beverage service.

There was a bit more activity going on now. People were either getting something out of the overheads or putting something back.

"Good morning … or afternoon, whatever it is," Mason said with a confused smile.

"Well, a good whatever it is to you as well," Cynthia replied. She did her best to fix herself up. *I must look awful*, she thought.

"I can't believe we only have an hour left." Mason reached into his wallet and took out his business card. He handed it over to Cynthia and said, "If you are ever in the market for quality antique furnishing or accent pieces, give me a call. I'll give you a great deal."

Cynthia took his card and said, "Well, thank you. I would love to visit your antique store and meet Uncle James and Aunt Emily."

"So Cynthia, since I already know your amazing life story, what is it you do for fun? Any hobbies or interests you didn't reveal in your story?" Mason asked.

"I do a lot of volunteer work at my church, mostly picnics and social outreaches. I like to read and watch very corny movies on my Christian movie channel. Oh, and I love shopping, mostly window-shopping though … on my budget," Cynthia replied. "I think I might like to travel, but so far I have mostly done it for work and not pleasure with the exception of the couple of weekend trips to Las Vegas and the Grand Canyon," Cynthia then said with a smile. "And how about you, Mason? What do you do for fun?"

"I love family get-togethers and functions, such as family picnics, weddings, birthdays, Christmas, or for just-whatever type occasions," Mason started. "I like to play softball, volleyball, go to the beach or pool for swimming, etc. I like going to the movies, attending live sporting events, or just watching sports on television. I like to run, bike, and go hiking. I guess I like to do a lot of things for fun when I find the time," Mason said with a smile.

Cynthia gathered a few things to go freshen up. "I'm going to head for the restroom and freshen up a little bit," Cynthia said to Mason.

"Sure," Mason said and stood up to let her out.

Before Mason sat back down, he glanced over at the gentleman sitting behind him. The man had a very soft and pleasant smile.

"Good morning," the gentleman said.

"Good morning," Mason replied and returned the friendly smile.

Wow, Mason thought. He couldn't believe this was the same guy who had been so very unpleasant at the beginning of the flight. Perhaps he was just tired or frustrated about traveling and leaving his family. Mason tried to never judge people based on a brief encounter. He wouldn't want to be judged by someone who really didn't have the opportunity to get to know him.

Just after he lost his wife, he wasn't always the friendliest guy to be around. And it wasn't anybody's fault that they didn't know he was just hurting.

This guy was definitely feeling better, and Mason was glad for him.

Chapter 12

Prepare for Landing

As both Cynthia and Mason thought about how much they had learned about each other, they both were amazed at how quickly this flight had flown by.

Both seemed sad and awkwardly quiet.

What does a person do after something like this?

Cynthia knew her statement in the beginning was, "We will never see each other again anyway."

That statement did not give her the same feeling it did now. It did not bring her comfort. She now wanted to see him again and often. She hoped to see him again and again and again.

And as Mason watched her prepare for landing, he realized he knew more about her than most of the people in his life.

In just these nine or so hours, she had shared so much of her life with him, and he had done the same.

How could he just say good-bye to her? How could she just say good-bye to him?

He felt emptiness and sadness as if he was losing or saying good-bye to a dear lifelong friend, one he knew he would never see again.

This was crazy and unbelievably ridiculous. He did not want to let her go.

He never thought he could ever be close to another woman again, and here he was … in love. Well, maybe not *in* love, but he knew he loved her.

In just nine hours? How could that be? Was it even possible?

He watched her every move, cherishing every moment. He knew he would never see her again. It was almost unbearable.

It reminded him a little of what he had felt when he had said his last good-bye to Lilly.

He needed to get a hold of himself.

Cynthia turned to him and smiled, "Well, this is it," she said.

Time just flew by. This was definitely the shortest trip she had ever experienced.

She tried to ignore the sadness she saw on his face. He looked like she felt.

He finally smiled back as if he realized she was reading his heart.

The captain's voice came over the speaker system. "Ladies and gentlemen, welcome to London. We are slightly behind schedule, and there may be a slight delay at our gate. We will be landing shortly. Please stay seated and make sure your seat belts are securely fastened."

Cynthia's connection was tight. She took the chance against her better judgment when she purchased her ticket.

As long as the wait for the gate is not too long, I can still make it, she thought to herself.

Mason wasn't worried about delays.

He always intentionally bought flights with long layovers, even next-day departures if the stop was near a known antique dealer. He had a five-and-a-half-hour layover in London on this flight.

He wasn't sure whether he would venture out this time, as he was a little tired from the trip. He really didn't sleep as much as he usually did. He didn't mind it at all though. He enjoyed the time he spent swapping stories with Cynthia and getting to know her.

"I sure hope you don't miss your connection," said Mason.

"Me too," Cynthia replied, "but if I do, I sure hope they can get me on another flight today. I really do need to be at the office tomorrow morning."

"I'm fine with my connection," Mason said. "I was thinking of going antique shopping, but I'm pretty drained. I think I will just freshen up, go find something to eat, and then find a cozy spot to wait for my flight."

"Ladies and gentlemen, we are now beginning our final descent into London Heathrow. The time is 11:25 a.m.," the captain announced.

The plane hit the tarmac firmly and raced down the runway. They had reached their destination together. Cynthia felt so lonely. She would miss Mason very much.

Mason didn't even want to look toward Cynthia as the plane came to a stop. All he could think of was that he was losing his best friend. He was going to miss her immensely. He wanted to know so much more about her.

The captain announced that it would be about twenty minutes or so before the gate was ready. He apologized for the delay and inconvenience that it would cause in regard to connections.

"Oh, well," Cynthia said. "I definitely missed my connection. I am so glad it is early. I shouldn't have a problem getting another flight to Milan for today."

"That's too bad you have to go through that trouble, but you're right. It's early, and you should not have a problem getting a new flight," Mason said.

"It could be worse," Cynthia said with a smile.

"You know, Cynthia, I really enjoyed our time together. This was like the best flight ever." He smiled. "You have my business card, so give me a call when you have some time," Mason said.

"I enjoyed this flight too, Mason," she replied. "It was actually … the best flight ever." They both smiled.

"And you have my business card too, so feel free to call me as well. Maybe I can swing by the antique shop sometime."

"That would be great!" Mason replied.

Both Mason and Cynthia started to feel a little better. It no longer seemed like this was good-bye forever.

Mason stood up to get his bag, but then he remembered it was a few rows back. He would have to wait until the people behind him went through. He asked Cynthia if she wanted to switch seats for now so that she could get a head start on getting a new flight to her destination.

"Sure," she said. He grabbed her bag for her from the overhead compartment and placed it on his seat. She came out of the row with her things, and he moved into the window seat with his things. The line still was not moving.

"I bet you're anxious to give Bryce a call," he said to Cynthia.

"I sure am. Probably as anxious as you are to call Tom," she replied.

"Yep, I already texted him," continued Mason. "I don't want to wake him. I think it's about 3:30 a.m. in California. I will wait a few hours to call him."

Finally the line started to move in the front. Mason looked at Cynthia and reached out his hand. Cynthia smiled and took his hand.

"Nice to have met you, Cynthia Ann Stewart," Mason said.

"Nice to have met you, Mason Thomas Scott," Cynthia replied.

"Take care," Mason continued.

"I will. You do the same," Cynthia responded. It was time for Cynthia to continue down the aisle and head for the exit. She let go of his hand slowly and reluctantly and headed to the airplane exit.

Chapter 13

Good-Bye?

As soon as she exited the plane, Cynthia went to the nearest service counter and asked how she could get another flight to Milan because she had missed her connection. The attendant directed her to the airline's customer service counter, which was about four gates down on the right-hand side.

"Thank you," Cynthia said to the attendant and proceeded hopefully toward the gate to get a new flight.

She couldn't stop thinking of Mason. If she didn't know any better, she would think she just fell in love with someone she had only known for ten or eleven hours. She looked back to see if she could see him and then continued to her destination.

Mason was so frustrated at his situation. He wished he and Cynthia could have walked off the plane together. It was taking forever to get off the plane.

As Mason stood anxiously waiting for all the passengers seated behind him to pass so he could get his bag, he thought of ways to catch up to Cynthia, to try to find her.

Mason noticed that the gentleman in the seat just behind him was still in his seat. When Mason glanced over toward him, their eyes met. The gentleman stood up and reached out his hand to Mason. Mason reached out his hand as well.

"Hi, I'm Robert Johnson," he said.

"Hi, I'm Mason Scott," Mason replied.

He seemed so gentle, a lot different than he seemed to be when he first got on the airplane.

"I want you to know I couldn't help but overhear the stories you and your friend shared," Robert began to tear up and cleared his throat.

Mason was a bit surprised at this.

"I saw myself, my wife, and my children in them, in your stories. It made me realize that my family deserves a better me, and I just want to thank you and your friend for helping me see that."

"That's great to know, Robert," Mason said.

"What overwhelms me the most is that I know God put me in seat 21C for a reason, and I will never forget this day—*never*." He began to cry softly.

Mason patted him on the shoulder and said, "We have all been there, Robert. No one is perfect. It takes a good man to admit the difference begins with him. Your family will truly be blessed."

By this time all the passengers had passed them. Mason hugged Robert and said, "God bless you, Robert, and your precious family. I'm always amazed at how God works."

Mason handed his business card to Robert and said, "Give me a call sometime. I'd like to know how things go."

"You bet I will, and God bless you too."

"I'll keep you in my prayers, my friend."

They shook hands, and Robert went on his way.

Mason grabbed his bag. He walked quickly to the plane exit, said thank you and good afternoon to the flight crew, and headed to the service desk.

He was so touched by Robert's words and transformation. He hoped he and his family would be blessed by his desire to be a better man, husband, and father.

He couldn't wait to tell Cynthia what had just happened. He hoped with all his heart that he would get the chance to do that.

"Hi, where would I go to rebook a flight for a missed connection," Mason asked the attendant.

The attendant directed Mason as he had Cynthia earlier.

Mason walked quickly toward the customer service desk. With great joy, he saw her standing in line. There were still a few people ahead of her. He quickly went into the men's restroom to freshen up.

When he came out, he saw her looking in the direction of gate 42, where they both had exited some time ago. Was she looking for him? He turned away for a minute to make sure he didn't bump into anyone as he attempted to make it across to approach her. He had no idea what he would say.

Immediately he heard her call out, "Mason!" He looked up, and she waved him over.

"Thank you, God," he said softly to himself as he picked up his bag and walked across toward her.

"So you finally made it off the plane," she said to him when he was close.

"Yes, I did, but there really isn't a big hurry for me. I'm stuck her for about five hours," Mason replied.

"Well, I'm praying that I can get a flight out as soon as possible. Five hours would be okay for me. I just hope they don't tell me I have to stay until tomorrow. I really need to be in the office tomorrow morning," Cynthia explained desperately.

Mason observed that Cynthia was very stressed and tired. "I'm sure you will get something sooner than that. They should have at least one seat available on a flight for today," Mason said, trying to comfort her.

He felt so helpless. He wanted to just make everything perfect for her … forever. He had not felt this obsessed with doing this for a person since his mother first and then Lilly. What was happening here … to him? Did he fall in love in ten hours? Could he or any other person for that matter fall in love in just ten hours? He attributed his thoughts and craziness to jet lag and fatigue.

"Next!" the customer service attendant called out.

Cynthia went to the desk and advised the attendant that she had missed her flight. She handed over her boarding pass and said she needed to get to Milan as soon as possible.

The attendant looked for flight options for a few minutes, but it seemed like hours to Cynthia, who stood still, barely breathing.

Mason had this tremendous urge to hug her and tell her everything was going to be just fine. She just looked like the type who always felt completely in charge and responsible, like no one ever took care of her the way he knew she deserved. She turned to him and smiled a sad, tired, worried smile that almost completely melted his heart.

"The soonest flight we have is at 4:25 p.m. today," the attendant informed her. "It will get you into Milan at 10:20 p.m. It makes one stop in Rome."

"I'll take it," she quickly replied. The attendant processed her ticket.

"Finally a happy smile," Mason said to Cynthia.

"I need to go to the ladies' room and freshen up a bit," she told Mason. "Then I should try to call Bryce."

"Do you want me to watch your bags while you go? I am going to send Tommy another text, and I will be right here," Mason offered.

"Sure, thanks. Then I will call Bryce when I get back," Cynthia said.

Cynthia went to the ladies' room, freshened up, and thought how lucky she was to get a flight out today. She also felt lucky to still have Mason. She felt as if she had known him all her life, like he was always a part of it and would always be. How could she let him go?

When she came out of the ladies' room, he was on the telephone with Tom. She could see the love he had for his son. It was absolutely amazing the loving expression and tone he used while he spoke with him.

She smiled at him and gestured that she was going to call Bryce.

He nodded his head in response.

Mason was so glad to hear Tommy's voice. He sounded happy to hear from him as well. Tom called immediately after he received Mason's second text. It surprised Mason, as he knew it had to be at least 4:30 a.m. or so in California.

"Hey, Dad, so you made it! How was the flight?" Tommy asked.

"It was actually a very good flight. The time just flew by. I am a bit tired though. I didn't sleep much on the plane like I usually do. I'll try to take a nap when I get settled in the hotel," Mason replied.

Mason thought it best not to tell Tommy about this new friend just yet. He would prefer to do it face-to-face after he got back home.

"Okay, son, I will let you go so you can get a little more sleep before you start your day. Thanks for calling. It's good to hear your voice. I will call you in your evening. I love you too. Bye, son." Mason hung up.

Cynthia texted Bryce. If he responded, she would give him a quick call. She realized it was around 4:30 a.m. in California. He may still be asleep. She just wanted him to know she made it safely. He would be worried if he didn't hear from her.

When she saw Mason hang up, she went over to where he was standing and watching over their bags.

"Well, Ms. Cynthia Ann Stewart, you must be hungry. Would you like to join me for lunch?" Mason asked.

"Actually that sounds terrific," she replied.

Mason and Cynthia ate at the Windsor Castle restaurant in terminal four. The waiter approached with some water and bread.

As he handed each of them the menus, he asked, "Would either of you like something else to drink?"

Mason looked over and gestured toward Cynthia so the waiter could take her order first.

Cynthia shyly said, "I would really like a glass of white wine or Zinfandel. Would that be okay with you, Mason?" She asked because she was never sure where some Christians stood on alcohol consumption, and she did not want to stumble or offend him.

"Of course," he replied to Cynthia. Then he looked at the waiter and said, "I will also have a glass. Thank you."

They both looked over the menu and decided what they wanted to order. When the waiter came back with their drinks, he took their food orders.

"I will have the fish and chips," Cynthia said.

As the waiter turned toward Mason, Mason said, "And I will have the pasta la pomodoro."

"Thank you," said the waiter as he took their menus.

"I can't believe we are already in London," Mason said to Cynthia. "You were right when you said that sharing our testimonies would make this trip fly by."

"Yes, mentally it flew by, but physically it was a very long trip. I am exhausted. However, I really did enjoy your company."

Mason grabbed his wine glass and raised it. He said, "Here's to a safe and very blessed flight for which I am very grateful for God's traveling mercies and a wonderful new friend," Mason toasted.

Cynthia clinked her glass against his and said, "Yes, salute and amen." They both smiled as they sipped the wine.

It was amazing how they interacted with each other. You would think they had been married for years. Talking about their sons and family, the plans they had when they finally got to their destination and work as well as what they had on their agendas when they arrived back home.

Mason told Cynthia about his chat with Robert Johnson and how much they both touched him with their stories. They were both pleased that God used them to minister to this gentleman.

Both Cynthia and Mason did a great job keeping themselves busy. It was probably to keep from getting lonely or realizing that they were indeed lonely.

They laughed and listened intensively to each other, so hungry to know everything about the other.

"You know, Mason, in all fairness there is a lot more to my story. You just got my perspective in a nutshell. I'm surely not perfect and possibly failed to share my imperfections. You know, there are two sides to every story," Cynthia explained.

Mason laughed and said, "Well, I'm sure I failed to share a few things myself. There really wasn't much time for details."

They both finished their meals. Neither of them realized how hungry they had been. Time was flying by. It was almost time for Cynthia to start heading for her gate. Both of them were so conscience of this.

The waiter brought the check, and Mason immediately grabbed it and took out his wallet to pay.

Cynthia took out her wallet as well.

"I got this," Mason said.

"Oh, no, Mason, I can pay for mine," Cynthia said.

Mason looked at Cynthia and said, "Please allow me the pleasure of at least treating you to lunch."

"Well, thank you, Mason. That is very nice of you," said Cynthia.

"My pleasure," Mason repeated.

I've got to do something here, Mason thought. *I've got to tell her how I'm feeling.* He knew he would regret it for the rest of his life if he didn't tell her, even if she thought he was crazy.

Finally Mason said, "Cynthia, I know you and I are both exhausted. We are probably both suffering from extreme jet lag, but I have to tell you I don't want this to end. I don't want to say good-bye and never see you again. I hope I'm not scaring you or out of line here. Forgive me if I am. I am not quite sure what is happening here, but I feel compelled to tell you what I feel."

Cynthia couldn't believe what she was hearing. He was saying everything she wanted to say to him but didn't have the courage to say.

He was so considerate and courageous in his communication. She knew it could not be easy for him to be so bold.

"Mason, you're not scaring me at all because I know what you are feeling. I feel the same way. We don't have to say good-bye, but we do have to get on with our trips. Let's agree to call and e-mail each other while we are out here when we can, although it will probably be a little difficult for me," Cynthia said.

"That sounds fantastic. I would really like that," Mason replied.

"I was also wondering whether you would consider the possibility of flying back home together at the end of your business trip." Mason carefully asked Cynthia. He hoped he hadn't gone too far with this request.

"How would we be able to do that? We are on different flights," Cynthia asked.

"I can meet you back here at London Heathrow on the day you are scheduled to be here. I can try to book a seat on your flight home," Mason explained.

"But what if we have to sit away from each other and we can't talk like we did?" Cynthia questioned.

"We can always ask a person to switch seats, or we can meet and chat periodically in the aisle.

Worst-case scenario is we will just end up back in Los Angeles together at the same time," Mason tried to plead his case.

"If you give me your flight details, I can try to make it work," Mason then said. "If this makes you feel uncomfortable at all, don't worry about it. We can always connect later back in Los Angeles. If you want to think about it, you can let me know later."

Mason wanted to make sure she didn't stress or feel pressured. The last thing he wanted to do was scare her away.

"Will you trust me?" Mason asked.

Cynthia was a bit overwhelmed. This was actually so much more than she had expected. *I mean really, he could be an ax murderer.* She had watched all those *Dateline* shows. He knew she was alone now.

Now she knew she was tired. Jet lag had definitely kicked in. Finally she replied, "I do trust you, Mason, but I'm a little overwhelmed here. As much as I feel I know everything about you, I really don't know anything at all for sure about you."

"Believe me, Cynthia, I am absolutely glad to hear you say that. I would want any woman I ever loved or cared about to be as smart and careful as you are being right now," Mason responded. "You have my cell number. Why don't you think about it? Google me, research me, whatever you have to do, and let me know later. You can even call my aunt and uncle if you'd like," he said and laughed.

Cynthia laughed as well.

He took out his airplane ticket and passport. "You see, I am Mason Thomas Scott. Take a picture with your cell phone. It has my birthday and address on it," Mason continued.

Cynthia took out her cell phone and snapped a couple of pictures. "You know, I'm a pretty good private eye," she said jokingly.

"Good!" Mason replied.

"So my extreme paranoia doesn't bother you?" Cynthia asked.

"You're not being paranoid. You're being smart. I respect that," Mason replied. "Cynthia Ann Stewart, somehow I know that if I have to be patient in getting to know you better and vice versa, it will be worth it," Mason said with a smile. "We'd better get you to your gate," Mason said quickly.

"Oh, yes, right. I don't want to miss this flight too!" Cynthia said as she gathered her belongings.

They both hurried along toward the gate. "Thanks again for having lunch with me," Mason said.

"My pleasure," Cynthia said.

They could hear the flight attendant announcing that they would begin boarding flight 207 to Milan.

Who was this woman who seemed to have taken his heart completely by surprise so unexpectedly? She was so sweet, smart, and beautiful. He knew deep down in his soul that only God could have made this possible. He also knew that there was so much more that they needed to learn about each other, and he was anxious to learn as much as possible. Hopefully she would call him.

The flight attendant called out for her group number.

"Well, that's me," she said. Mason looked into her soft, tired eyes and smiled. He took her hand and said, "It was a pleasure meeting you," and then he lifted her hand to his lips and kissed it softly. She smiled and began to feel her tears but took a deep breath.

They looked at each other for a while as if they didn't know what to do. They both giggled, and Mason kissed her on her forehead and hugged her.

"God bless you and have a safe trip. Send me a text if you get a chance."

"I will," she said.

She grabbed her things and went through the gate. She didn't dare look back. The tears she had tried so hard to hold back were streaming down her face. She didn't want Mason to see her crying.

She would miss him dearly. Was he a dream? He was everything she had ever dreamed of—handsome, kind, caring, loving, and just such a gentlemen. He was a very nice Christian man.

There it is, Mason thought. *That familiar feeling I haven't felt in more than fifteen hours—loneliness.* He went to his gate to wait for his flight to depart. He could only hope that he would see her again someday.

Chapter 14

The Decision

Cynthia immediately researched Mason Thomas Scott on her computer when she arrived at her hotel in Milan. Listings for the antique shop came up on her computer screen as well as a website address. She would most definitely call Aunt Emily and Uncle James tonight, which would be their morning.

"Paulson's Antique Shoppe, may I help you?"

"Hello, my name is Cynthia. I am a friend of Mason's, and I was hoping to speak with James or Emily Paulson."

"This is James Paulson," he said.

"Oh, hello, Uncle James … I mean, Mr. Paulson. I was just checking to see what time your store in Westwood opens," Cynthia asked.

"It opens at 9:00 a.m., but I am afraid that Mason will not be there. He is currently on his annual trip to Europe," Uncle James explained.

"Oh, I see. When do you expect him back?" Cynthia asked.

"He is expected to return on Friday. However, I am not sure whether he will be in the shop on Saturday or not. Would you like for me to have him call you?" Uncle James offered.

"Oh, no, thank you. I will call back after he returns. Thank you so much for your help," Cynthia answered.

"You are very welcome. Bye now," Uncle James replied.

"Good-bye," Cynthia replied with a smile and hung up.

Cynthia continued to search the Internet for additional information, remembering some of the names of family members Mason mentioned in his stories.

Mason grabbed his bag and looked around his hotel room to make sure he had everything. He had slept very well last night and hoped that Cynthia had made it to Milan safely.

He made his way toward the elevator, wondering whether he should grab a quick breakfast after he checked out or just wait to grab something when he got near this client's office, which was located near the Colosseum.

His appointment was at 10:00 a.m. It would last at least three hours. Afterward, he would look around at other local shops.

Mason couldn't get Cynthia off his mind. He wished that she could have accompanied him on his trip. It would have been nice to have someone to share Rome with.

His flight to Paris, France, would depart at 7:45 p.m. tonight. His plan was to stay in Paris until Thursday evening and fly back to London for his return flight home on Friday morning. Better yet, on Thursday if Cynthia decided to take him up on his plan to fly back together.

It would be so lonesome without Cynthia if she decided it would be better to wait until they got back to California to connect. He decided he would try to call her Tuesday evening just to hear her voice.

His meeting in Rome was with Carlo Poletti, an antique dealer his uncle had dealt with for years. He seemed to always know exactly what they were looking for. He had a few pieces out he felt Mason would be interested in. There were a few very unique vases and a couple of glass bowls. As always there were a few additional items that caught Mason's eye as well. Mason selected the items he wished to purchase and asked Carlo to ship them to his uncle's store in San Bernardino.

Carlo and Mason went to a local restaurant for lunch. Afterward, Mason said good-bye to Carlo and headed for a few old antique shops located just outside of Rome. Mason didn't find anything that interested him.

It was now around 4:30 p.m., so he decided to head for the airport. All of a sudden his phone beeped. *Probably a text from Tom*, he thought.

He pulled out his phone and clicked on the text.

His heart stopped. It was a copy of Cynthia's flight information for her return flight.

"Yes! Thank you, God. Thank you. Thank you so much!"

His evening was going to be a lot different and busier than he had planned. He would immediately start working on their flights as soon as he got to the airport.

There was absolutely nothing that was going to prevent him from making sure he and Cynthia were together on their return flight.

Absolutely nothing, he thought adamantly.

Printed in the United States
By Bookmasters